Colombia

NATIONS OF THE MODERN WORLD: LATIN AMERICA

Ronald Schneider, *Series Editor*

Colombia: Democracy Under Assault,
Second Edition, Harvey F. Kline

†*Cuba: Dilemmas of a Revolution,*
Third Edition, Juan M. del Aguila

Bolivia: Land of Struggle, Waltraud Queiser Morales

†*The Dominican Republic: A Caribbean Crucible,*
Second Edition, Howard J. Wiarda and Michael J. Kryzanek

Nicaragua: The Land of Sandino,
Third Edition, Thomas W. Walker

Venezuela: Tarnished Democracy, Daniel C. Hellinger

Paraguay: The Personalist Legacy,
Riordan Roett and Richard Scott Sacks

Haiti: The Breached Citadel, Patrick Bellegarde-Smith

Mexico: Paradoxes of Stability and Change,
Second Edition, Daniel Levy and Gabriele Székely

FORTHCOMING

†*Brazil: Culture and Politics in
a New Industrial Powerhouse,* Ronald Schneider

Peru, Gregory D. Schmidt

†Available in hardcover and paperback

SECOND EDITION

COLOMBIA
Democracy
Under Assault

HARVEY F. KLINE

WestviewPress
A Division of HarperCollins*Publishers*

Nations of the Modern World: Latin America

Map 1.1 is from Howard J. Wiarda and Harvey F. Kline, *Latin American Politics and Development*, 3rd ed. (Boulder: Westview Press, 1990).

Copyright © 1983, 1995 by Westview Press, Inc., A Division of HarperCollins Publishers, Inc.

Published in 1995 in the United States of America by Westview Press, Inc., 5500 Central Avenue, Boulder, Colorado 80301-2877, and in the United Kingdom by Westview Press, 12 Hid's Copse Road, Cumnor Hill, Oxford OX2 9JJ

Library of Congress Cataloging-in-Publication Data
Kline, Harvey F.
  Colombia: democracy under assault / Harvey F. Kline. — 2nd ed.
    p. cm.—(Nations of the modern world. Latin America)
  Includes bibliographical references and index.
  ISBN 0-8133-1071-7
    1. Colombia—Politics and government—1930–1946. 2. Colombia—
Politics and government—1946–1974. 3. Colombia—Politics and
government—1974– 4. Democracy—Colombia—History—20th century.
5. Colombia—Economic conditions. 6. Drug traffic—Colombia—
History—20th century. 7. Violence—Colombia—History—20th
century. 8. Colombia—Relations—Foreign countries. I. Title.
II. Series.
F2277.K55   1995
986.106'3—dc20   95-8136
                                                                      CIP

Printed and bound in the United States of America

The paper used in this publication meets the requirements of the American National Standard for Permanence of Paper for Printed Library Materials Z39.48-1984.

10   9   8   7   6   5   4   3   2   1

Dedicated to Colombians who want to join together—
despite differences of race, religion, gender, region,
or class—to bring their beautiful country
out of one hundred years
of violence

Before reaching the final line, however, he had already understood that he would never leave that room, for it was foreseen that the city of mirrors (or mirages) would be wiped out by the wind and exiled from the memory of men at the precise moment when Aureliano Babilonia would finish deciphering the parchments, and that everything written on them was unrepeatable since time immemorial and forever more, because races condemned to one hundred years of solitude did not have a second opportunity on earth.

—Gabriel García Márquez,
One Hundred Years of Solitude

Contents

1 THE LAND AND THE PEOPLE   1

Geographical Variation and Regionalism, 1
Social Distinctions, 9
Modernization, 22
Conclusion, 24
Notes, 24

2 COLOMBIA FROM PREHISTORY TO 1930   26

The Spanish Colony, 28
Independence and Gran Colombia, 29
The First Century of Colombian Independence, 30
Conclusion, 37
Notes, 38

3 PARTISAN CONFLICT, 1930–1974   40

Conflict and Violence, 1930–1958, 40
The National Front, 1958–1974, 47
Conclusion, 52
Notes, 53

4 THE EDGE OF CHAOS, 1974–1994   55

Guerrillas, 57
Drugs, 59

5 GOVERNMENT AND POLITICS   68

6 THE COLOMBIAN MIXED ECONOMY AND PUBLIC POLICY   93

7 THE INTERNATIONAL DIMENSION   115

8 PROGNOSIS   131

Tables and Illustrations

Acronyms

ACOLFA Asociación Colombiana de Fabricantes de Autopartes (Colombian Association of Automobile Parts Manufacturers)

ACOPI Asociación Colombiana de Pequeños Industriales (Colombian Association of Small Industrialists)

ACOPLASTICOS Asociación Colombiana de Industrias Plásticas (Colombian Association of Plastics Industries)

AD-M19 Alianza Democrática M-19 (M-19 Democratic Alliance)

ADPOSTAL Administración Postal Nacional (National Postal Administration)

AID Agency for International Development

ANALDEX Asociación Nacional de Exportadores (National Association of Exporters)

ANAPO Alianza Nacional Popular (National Popular Alliance)

ANDI Asociación Nacional de Industriales (National Association of Industrialists)

ANIF Asociación de Instituciones Financieras (National Association of Financial Institutions)

ANUC Asociación Nacional de Usuarios Campesinos (National Association of Peasants)

ASOBANCARIA Asociación Bancaria de Colombia (Colombian Bankers' Association)

ASOCAÑA Asociación de Productores y Exportadores de Caña de Azucar (Association of Sugarcane Producers and Exporters)

CAMACOL Cámara Colombiana de Construcción (Colombian Chamber of Construction)

CARBOCOL Carbones de Colombia (Colombian Coal Company)

CAT *certificado de abono tributario* (a general tax-credit certificate)

CGT Confederación General de Trabajo (General Confederation of Labor)

COLCIENCIAS Fondo Colombiano de Investigaciones Científicas y Proyectos Especiales (Colombian Fund for Scientific Investigations and Special Projects)

COLCULTURA Instituto Colombiano de Cultura (Colombian Institute of Culture)

COLDEPORTES Instituto Colombiano de la Juventud y el Deporte (Colombian Institute of Youth and Sport)

COLPUERTOS Empresa Puertos de Colombia (Colombian Port Enterprise)

CONPES Consejo Nacional de Política Económica y Social (National Council of Economic and Social Policy)

CRIC Consejo Regional Indígena del Cauca (Regional Indigenous Council of the Cauca)

CSTC Confederación Sindical de Trabajadores de Colombia (Workers' Union Confederation of Colombia)

CTC Confederación de Trabajadores Colombianos (Confederation of Colombian Workers)

DNP Departamento Nacional de Planeación (National Planning Department)

ECLA Economic Council for Latin America
ECOMINAS Empresa Colombiana de Minas (Colombian Mining Enterprise)
ECOPETROL Empresa Colombiana de Petróleos (Colombian Petroleum Enterprise)
ELN Ejército de Liberación Nacional (National Liberation Army)
EPL Ejército Popular de Liberación (People's Liberation Army)
FARC Fuerzas Armadas Revolucionarias Colombianas (Revolutionary Armed Forces of
    Colombia)
FASECOLDA Unión de Aseguradores Colombianos (Union of Colombian Insurers)
FEDECAFE Federación Nacional de Cafeteros (National Federation of Coffee Growers)
FEDEGAN Federación Nacional de Ganaderos (National Federation of Livestock Raisers)
FEDEMETAL Federación Colombiana de Industrias Metalúrgicas (Colombian
    Federation of Metallurgical Industries)
FENALCO Federación Nacional de Comerciantes (National Federation of Merchants)
FFCC Ferrocarriles Nacionales de Colombia (National Railroads of Colombia)
GDP gross domestic product
HIMAT Instituto Colombiano de Hidrología, Meteorología, y Adecuación de Tierras
    (Colombian Institute of Hydrology, Meteorology, and Land Improvement)
ICBF Instituto Colombiano de Bienestar Familiar (Colombian Institute of Family
    Welfare)
ICEL Instituto Colombiano de Energía Eléctrica (Colombian Institute of Electrical
    Energy)
ICFES Instituto Colombiano para el Fomento de la Educación Superior (Colombian
    Institute for the Promotion of Higher Education)
ICSS Instituto Colombiano de los Seguros Sociales (Colombian Institute of Social
    Security)
ICT Instituto de Crédito Territorial (Institute of Land Credit)
IDB Inter-American Development Bank
IFI Instituto de Fomento Industrial (Industrial Promotion Institute)
IMF International Monetary Fund
INCOMEX Instituto Colombiano de Comercio Exterior (Colombian Institute of Foreign
    Commerce)
INCORA Instituto Colombiano de la Reforma Agraria (Colombian Agrarian Reform
    Institute)
INDERENA Instituto de Desarrollo de Recursos Naturales Renovables y del Ambiente
    (Institute for the Development of Renewable Natural Resources and of the
    Environment)
INGEOMINAS Instituto Nacional de Investigaciones Geológicas-Mineras (National
    Institute of Geological Mining Investigations)
INRAVISION Instituto Nacional de Radio y Televisión (National Institute of Radio and
    Television)
INTERCOR International Colombia Resources Corporation
INTRA Instituto Nacional de Transporte (National Institute of Transportation)
LAFTA Latin American Free Trade Association
MAS Muerte a Secuestradores (Death to Kidnappers)
M-19 Movimiento 19 de Abril (19th of April Movement)
MRL Movimiento Revolucionario Liberal (Revolutionary Liberal Movement)

MSN Movimiento de Salvación Nacional (National Salvation Movement)
NFD Nueva Fuerza Democrática (New Democratic Force)
OAS Organization of American States
OPEC Organization of Petroleum Exporting Countries
PCC Partido Comunista Colombiano (Colombian Communist Party)
PRI Partido Revolucionario Institucional (Revolutionary Institutional Party)
PROEXPO Fondo de Promoción de Exportaciones (Export Promotion Fund)
SAC Sociedad de Agricultores de Colombia (Colombian Agriculturists' Society)
SENA Servicio Nacional de Aprendizaje (National Apprenticeship Service)
SENDAS Secretariado Nacional de Asistencia Social (National Secretariat of Social
    Assistance)
TELECOM Empresa Nacional de Telecomunicaciones (National Telecommunications
    Enterprise)
UFCO United Fruit Company
UN United Nations
UP Unión Patriótica (Patriotic Union)
UPAC *unidades de poder adquisitivo constante* (units of constant buying power)
UTC Unión de Trabajadores Colombianos (Union of Colombian Workers)

Preface

IN THE FIRST EDITION OF THIS BOOK, published in 1983, I was writing about a South American country that most citizens of the United States knew little about. Now, however, Colombia is often in the news, for it exports some 80 percent of the cocaine consumed in the United States. The purpose of this new edition is to introduce readers to a complex and beautiful country that in the past dozen years has been transformed from a fairly successful democracy to a near-pariah. My thesis is straightforward: Colombia has become a country in which homicide is the leading cause of death as a result of decisions made by its political, economic, and social leaders, some of them dating to its earliest days of independence.

Perhaps more than any other country in Latin America, Colombia has always proved puzzling to outsiders. Marxists have been frustrated by the tendency for competition between the two traditional political parties to be more important than social class conflict; liberal democrats have found it hard to understand why a country with so many of the trappings of liberal democracy often does not act like one. Students of the politics of other Latin American countries have been surprised not to find it a praetorian state similar to those common in the Southern Cone and wondered why the corporatism brought to the New World by the Spanish is weak if not nonexistent. Most recently, people in the United States have asked themselves how it is possible, if Colombia is a democracy, for it to be the world's major producer of cocaine.

In this attempt to describe Colombia today, several general themes emerge: that we must set aside preconceptions and allow Colombia to speak for itself; that its people are facing all of the very serious and perhaps increasing problems of living in a developing country; and that in a sense "Colombia" exists only in popular myth, academic reification, World Cup soccer and the Olympic Games, and the assemblies of international organizations. In the end, I will not be able to explain fully why Colombia has taken the route it has; there is no easy answer to this question. I hope, nevertheless, that this new edition will give readers a better understanding of the country, its prospects, and its problems.

I would be remiss if I did not thank those who have made this project possible. I have conducted more than one hundred confidential interviews in Colombia over the past years. At appropriate places they are cited in this book. During my eight trips to Colombia (where I have lived for four and a half years out of the last thirty), many organizations and literally hundreds of persons have helped me to understand the country. Space allows me to mention only a few: the Fulbright-Hays Commission (which funded two research trips) and its director, Francisco Gnecco Calvo; Latin American Teaching Fellowships; the Research Council of the University of Massachusetts at Amherst; the University of North Carolina at Chapel Hill; and the scores of Colombian politicians who have given me time over the years. I thank especially my colleagues and good friends in the Departamento de Ciencia Política at the Universidad de los Andes: Dora Rothlisberger, Francisco Leal, Gabriel Murillo, Magdalena León, and Armando and Rocío Borrero, who have all contributed greatly to this book. Jaime Bonilla, of the Departamento de Ingeniería of the Universidad de los Andes, kindly responded to my request for data on coffee exports. Vanessa Gray, a former student, helped update the data in Chapter 6. My thanks go to Eduardo Pizarro and his colleagues at the Instituto de Estudios Políticos at the Universidad Nacional.

I am grateful to the United States Institute of Peace (USIP) for a grant that made it possible for me to return to Bogotá in 1991, 1992, and 1994. This grant allowed me to be in Bogotá for the end of the Constituent Assembly, the surrender of Pablo Escobar (and later his escape from prison), the government's conversations with two guerrilla groups in Caracas, and the first round of the 1994 presidential election.

I would also like to thank those in the United States who read earlier versions of this book and whose comments helped to make it better: Daniel Premo of Washington College; Jonathan Hartlyn of the University of North Carolina at Chapel Hill; Edward Epstein of the University of Utah; Jay Meeks and Leigh Aldrop, graduate students at the University of Alabama; Helen Delpar and Richard Diehl, colleagues at the University of Alabama; the editors at Johns Hopkins University Press; and Ronald Schneider, general editor of the Westview Press series Nations of the Modern World: Latin America. Special appreciation goes to my wife, Dottie, who not only spent three years in Colombia with me but also has been a critic, editor, and helper with this book in both of its editions. I, however, am entirely responsible for all of its contents.

I trust that Colombians will accept my assessment of their country not as some sort of North American imperialism but as the best judgment of one who cares for it deeply. I finished this book listening to my latest treasures from Bogotá, *Las Cién Canciones Más Bellas de Colombia* and *Las 100 Canciones Más Bailables de Colombia*, sometimes pausing to sing along with "Antioqueñita," "Navidad Negra," or "La Banda Borracha." My fondest hope is that I will see the day when Colombia has recognized that the fault is not in its stars and has left behind its more than one hundred years of violence.

Harvey F. Kline

1

THE LAND
AND THE PEOPLE

Colombia, at the northwest corner of South America, covers 1,141,748 square kilometers (440,829 square miles), two-thirds again the area of the state of Texas. With Venezuela and Brazil to the east, Ecuador to the south, and Panama to the west, it is both a Caribbean country and one with a long Pacific coastline. Its 35 million people make it the third-most-populous Latin American country, ranking behind only Brazil and Mexico.

Geographical Variation and Regionalism

Colombia includes the Andes mountains, the tropical rain forest of the Amazon jungle, the grasslands of the Orinoco River, and other tropical rain forests on both the Caribbean and Pacific coasts. The whole of the country is in the Tropics between 12° north latitude and 4° south latitude (see map). This means that length-of-day variations by time of year are slight, but it does not mean that all parts of Colombia are alike climatically or geographically or that all are hot. Rather, climate varies with altitude. In the Andes, for example, in an hour's drive one can travel from a cool area where potatoes are the major crop to a warm one where coffee and bananas are grown. Mean temperature ranges from 28° C (82° F), corresponding to summer in Washington, D.C., to 13° C, the temperature of a southern New England spring. Indeed, the argument has been made that one reason national economic integration did not come sooner to Colombia was that the diversity of crops available near the major cities made trade unnecessary.

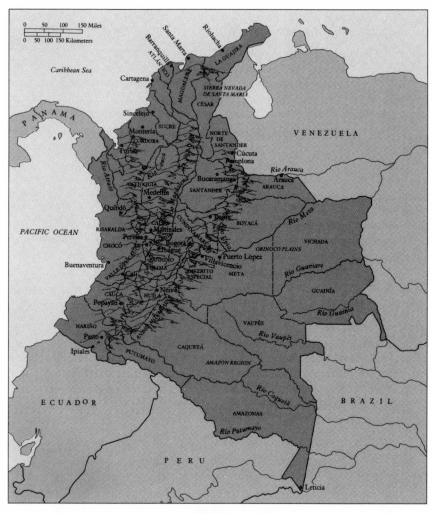

Colombia

The Andes mountain range splits near the border with Ecuador into three major cordilleras that continue north all the way to Venezuela. The mountains are higher than the U.S. Rockies, and until the advent of air transportation in the 1930s travel between the regions was difficult and time-consuming. Even today a trip from Bogotá to Medellín, half an hour away by jet, takes at least eight hours by bus. The western range is the lowest of the three; although its highest peak is 4,400 meters (14,436 feet), a number of others are between 3,600 and 4,000 meters (from 11,811 to 13,123 feet). The central range is the highest, with a number of permanently snow-covered peaks (despite their being less than 4° from the equator), the highest of which is Sierra Nevada del Huila at 5,429 meters (17,812

Neusa, near Bogotá, in Andean Colombia (Photo by Andrés Rothstein, reprinted by permission.)

The Amazon (Photo by Andrés Rothstein, reprinted by permission.)

feet). The eastern range is somewhat lower on average than the central, although its highest peak (5,493 meters or 18,022 feet) is higher than any in the central. The eastern is both the longest and the widest of the three ranges. The highest peaks in Colombia are, however, not in the Andes but in the Sierra Nevada, where the Colón and Bolívar peaks are 5,775 meters (18,947 feet) high. On a clear day, these peaks are visible from the Caribbean beaches of Santa Marta.

Most authorities agree that the three major regions in Colombia are the East, the Andean, and the Caribbean, but because the Andes form such formidable barriers, there is much disagreement about subregions. In this book I follow the four-region division shown in Table 1.1.[1]

The Andean Regions

The most important events in Colombia's history have taken place in the Andes. It is there that the most complex Amerindian societies developed, that the Spanish

TABLE 1.1   Major Characteristics of Colombian Regions

| | *Percentage of National* | | |
Region	Territory	Population	Industry
Central Andean	8.6	37.6	36.4
Western Andean	21.9	35.2	51.1
Caribbean Coast	11.6	20.0	12.0
East	57.8	7.2	0.5

SOURCES: *Atlas básico de Colombia* (Bogotá: Instituto Geográfico "Agustín Codazzi," 1980), 80–133; *Colombia Today*, 24, 1 (1989): 2–5.

established the major city of the area, Santafé de Bogotá, and that most Colombians have traditionally lived (about 75 percent of the people live there to-day—probably the lowest proportion of the population in recent centuries). In addition, most industrial and political activities have taken place there. Until the recent growth of the Caribbean coast, this 30 percent portion of the country's territory was, for all intents and purposes, "Colombia."

Some parts of the Andes (for example, Nariño and the Cundiboyacense area) historically had large Indian populations, while others—intermountain valleys that were warm enough for sugarcane cultivation (Valle del Cauca) and contained gold deposits (Antioquia, Chocó)—had relatively few Indians and saw the introduction of large numbers of African slaves. Still other areas (such as the Santanderes) where the number of Indians was small supported the development of small farms and artisan industries.

The Central Andean. Except during the nineteenth-century federal period, the Central Andean region has always been the governmental and administrative center of the country. In addition, this area is characterized by agriculture that varies with elevation: cultivation of potatoes and grains on the plains of Bogotá, at 2,600 meters (8,530 feet), and Boyacá; tobacco in the Santanderes; and corn, coffee, and citrus fruits at lower elevations.

The capital, Santafé de Bogotá (as it is officially called according to the Constitution of 1991), is in the Central Andean region. Although Bogotá does not compare in size or in percentage of the nation's population with some of the other metropolises of Latin America, it has grown rapidly in recent decades (50 percent from 1973 to 1980 and from 350,000 to more than 6 million in the past fifty years). Bogotá is by far the largest Colombian city, with a full 17 percent of the national population, and has a cool, vernal climate. The original population was Indian, white, and a mixture of the two (mestizo). Today, because of in-migration from all parts of the country, Bogotanos are physically much more diverse, and many speak with their regional accents. Although the city was not the original industrial center of Colombia, during the past thirty

Bogotá, near the center of the capital of six million people (Photo courtesy of the Organization of American States.)

years manufacturing establishments have moved into the area because of its abundance of low-priced labor. Most of the employed, however, work in other sectors of the economy, especially services. Bogotá celebrated its 450th anniversary in 1988, and many of the buildings in its center, including the National Cathedral and the La Candelaria residential section, date from the seventeenth century.

The Western Andean. The Western Andean region includes the northwestern department of Antioquia, whose capital, Medellín, is the second-largest city in Colombia and the country's original industrial center. Today 63 percent of Colombia's textile industry is in Medellín, including the oldest and largest company in that field, Coltejer. Antioquia is also a major coffee-producing area, along with Caldas, Quindiío, and Risaralda, all in the Western Andean region. The region also contains the sugarcane-growing Valle del Cauca. As the center of this prosperous sugarcane area, Cali, the third-largest Colombian city, plays an important role in the national economy. The two major cocaine-exporting groups are centered in Medellín and Cali. Valle has a large black population, and so does the gold mining department of Chocó. Slaves were imported to the region to supplement Indian labor in gold mining, and consequently whites, blacks, mestizos (white-Indian), mulattos white-black), *zambos* (Indian-black) and occasionally pure Indians can be found there. *La raza antioqueña* (the Antioquian race), as the inhabitants proudly call themselves, is light-skinned. The Western Andean region (especially Antioquia and the areas populated by Antioqueño migration in the nineteenth century) was traditionally one of the fastest-growing regions, mainly because of the tendency toward large families. Since 1973, however, the region's population has been growing more slowly than that of the nation as a whole.

Antioqueños are known in other parts of Colombia for their distinctive work ethic. Instead of spending most of their earnings for consumption, it is said, Antioqueños save their money to reinvest in land to grow more coffee, factories, or, more recently, facilities for producing cocaine. Colombians' explanations for this vary. One of them is that the Antioqueños are descended from Sephardic Jewish refugees from the Spanish Inquisition. In his pathbreaking investigation, James Parsons rejects this idea, pointing to the absence of any such suggestion in the historical records from that period. He stresses that the myth spread because of its use by novelists and poets and suggests that "the popular acceptance of the legend is clearly related to a feeling of inferiority which seems to exist among other Colombian groups, envious of the economic successes and the 'Yankee materialism' of the Antioqueños."[2] Another explanation traces the Antioqueños to the north of Spain instead of Castille or Andalucía, and still another points to the isolation of the region. Colombians from elsewhere at once admire Antioqueños for their economic successes and criticize them for not sharing their own more relaxed attitudes, but they are beginning to follow their example.[3]

Popayán, colonial city of churches (Photo by Andrés Rothstein, reprinted by permission.)

The southern part of the Western Andean region has less industry and population than the rest of the region but makes up for this in territory. The area is agricultural, with variations in crops, as in other Andean regions, according to elevation. Pereira, with a population of 390,000, is its largest city. Popayán, an important city during colonial times and in the nineteenth century, now comes to life during Holy Week each year, when thousands of Colombian and foreign tourists come to watch the religious processions, purportedly second in their splendor only to those of Seville. The population of the Tolima area is much like that of the Central Andean region, a combination of white, indigenous, and mestizo. The southeastern area, however, has large numbers of Indians, some of whom maintain their traditional dress, crafts, and languages.

The Caribbean Coast

The Caribbean coastal region (the Costa Atlántica) has in recent years been the area that has grown most rapidly (by 25 percent between 1973 and 1980, for example, when the entire country grew by 21 percent). The climate is hot, and tropical diseases such as gastroenteritis and malaria are common, but recent medical and technological advances, as well as the drug trade, commerce, and a new coal industry, are bringing this area into greater prominence. Barranquilla, Colombia's major port and fourth-largest city, is a major industrial center. During the 1980s large coal mines were opened up in the El Cerrejón area of La Guajira, while marijuana became an important export from the region around Santa Marta. The Caribbean region has large numbers of people descended from the African slaves imported for plantation agriculture. Indeed, Cartagena was the major slave port for all of Spanish South America. At the same time, the many Indians and whites contribute to the coast's distinctive racial mix.

The East

The East has two distinct subregions. The southern, which consists of tropical rain forest, is part of the Amazon Basin. Rubber was an important product in the early 1900s; now the region is most important for tourism, the export of animals to zoos, and the growing of coca and the production of cocaine. The north of the region is part of the Orinoco Basin, an area of grasslands with seasonal flooding, rather than a tropical rain forest. Livestock grazing is the most important economic activity, although some crops are grown (rice, for example, and recently coca). These eastern plains are the "cowboy" part of Colombia—horses often provide transportation and the carrying of sidearms is not uncommon.

Social Distinctions

Added to the regional diversity of Colombia is a distinctive social class system based on income, race, and gender. Since Colombia is both a Caribbean and an Andean country, it contains social distinctions common to countries of Central America and the Caribbean as well as those more in keeping with patterns in other Andean countries.

Income Distribution

Economic inequality, linked with both race and gender, is the most salient characteristic of Colombian society and many Colombian leaders consider it the primary cause of violence. Signs of the inequitable distribution of income are everywhere. Although the percentage of Colombians living in poverty has decreased in recent decades (40 percent of the population in 1991 as compared with some 70 percent thirty years earlier), poverty is now more visible in the cities. In 1988, the

TABLE 1.2   Income Distribution in Colombia, 1938–1988

			Decile		
Year	1–5 (Poor)	6–8 (Middle)	9 (Upper Middle)	10 (Upper)	Gini Coefficient
1938	20.0	28.8	16.3	34.9	0.45
1951	16.7	24.7	15.1	43.5	0.53
1964	14.8	24.2	15.5	45.5	0.55
1971	16.1	25.8	16.2	42.0	0.53
1978	18.6	27.8	16.0	37.6	0.48
1988	18.9	28.2	15.9	37.1	0.48

SOURCE: Juan Luis Londoño, "Distribución nacional del ingreso en 1988: Una mirada en perspectiva," *Coyuntura Social,* no. 1, 1989, quoted in José Antonio Ocampo, "Reforma del Estado y desarrollo económico y social en Colombia," *Análisis Político,* no. 17 (1992), 26.

lowest 50 percent of the population received only 18.9 percent of the income, while the top 10 percent had almost twice that much, 37.1 percent (Table 1.2). What this means for many Colombians, according to a 1983 study, is that 54 percent of the households had monthly incomes below US$200, and households in the lowest quintile spent more than their total official income for food alone.[4]

The same imbalance is seen in the ownership of land. In 1960, 62.5 percent of all agricultural landholdings were less than 5 hectares (12.3 acres), and these plots occupied only 4.5 percent of all agricultural land. At the other extreme, 0.07 percent of landholdings were greater than 2,500 hectares (6,173 acres), making up 20.2 percent of all agricultural land. In 1970–1971, after more than a decade of agrarian reform, there were fewer very small plots but also more holdings of more than 2,500 hectares.[5] Since then, land reform has not been a priority of Colombian governments and land may be even more inequitably distributed than ever. With the new violence of leftist guerilla groups and paramilitaries, some landowners have fled to the cities. At the same time, drug dealers have bought land to grow coca, to be "gentleman farmers," and to launder their drug profits.

Race

No recent Colombian census has included questions about race, and the absence of agreement about the physical characteristics associated with the many combinations in the Colombian gene pool has meant that race is not a factor examined in public opinion polls. Nor is there enough agreement to make self-identification valid.[6] The figures for races in Colombia assembled by the U.S. State Department and the U.S. Central Intelligence Agency are only guesswork. The national racial order is based on "the contradictory but interdependent coexistence of blackness, indianness, mixedness, and whiteness."[9]

Indian family in Amazon jungle (Photo by Andrés Rothstein, reprinted by permission.)

In general, race seems of relatively little importance in the daily lives of Colombians. No laws have ever been passed to end discrimination by race simply because no laws allowing discrimination ever existed. Voting in Colombia has never been restricted by race (although the literacy requirement in place until the 1930s did affect people of color more than whites), and almost all citizens have participated in politics since very early in Colombian history, albeit in quite different ways.

This is not, however, to say that there is no racial prejudice. Peter Wade suggests that Colombian race relations be visualized as a triangle whose uppermost point

Middle-class children near Bogotá (Photo by Andrés Rothstein, reprinted by permission.)

is white and whose bottom corners are black and Indian. According to Wade, the white apex is associated with power, wealth, civilization, government, and high degrees of urbanity, education, and culture. The bottom two corners are seen from the top as primitive, dependent, uneducated, rural, and inferior. Blacks are stereotyped as lazy, as having an abnormal family structure because of an absence of males to provide role models, and as loving music, dancing, and celebration. Indians are perceived by whites as even more foreign and distinct, especially in lifestyle and language.[8]

The poor in Bogotá, living in a shanty near a luxury apartment building (Photo by Harvey F. Kline.)

According to the archconservative Laureano Gómez, president from 1949 to 1953, "Our race comes from the mixture of Spaniards, indians and blacks. The latter two flows of heritage are marks of complete inferiority. It is in whatever we have been able to inherit from the Spanish spirit that we must look for the guiding lines of the contemporary Colombian character."[9] In more general terms, the system is one of *blanqueamiento* (whitening), valuing whiteness and disparaging blackness and Indianness.[10] In the almost complete absence of systematic studies of this phenomenon, anecdotal information must suffice. A friend once told me that when he was growing up in northeastern Cúcuta, it was an advantage for him to have curly hair: in an indigenous area it distinguished him from a racial group characterized by straight hair. Later, when his family moved to Cali, where many African slaves had been brought to work on the plantations, his formerly desirable curly hair became undesirable, as it clearly suggested that he might have black ancestry. An Antioqueña of Spanish background remarked in my hearing that, after a week in the sun, she was beginning to look like an *india*. The writer Andrés Hurtado, of Quimbaya background, has argued that Colombia will progress only when calling someone an *indio* is no longer an insult but a compliment.[11]

There is a strong correlation between race and social class. Most members of the upper class are white. Many members of the working class are people of color. Clearly, other things being equal it is more advantageous to be white. Given the

The poor in Bogotá, a homeless woman (Photo by Andrés Rothstein, reprinted by permission.)

opportunity, however, persons of color can join a "whiter" group by changing their lifestyle. In the highlands of Cundinamarca and Boyacá, for example, individuals of pure indigenous background may not be considered *indios* because they dress as others do and speak Spanish rather than an indigenous language. Similarly, people racially of pure African-American heritage may pursue a "social whitening" by living in cities and becoming integrated into nonblack networks. How this process occurs varies from region to region.[12]

Indígenas (as Colombians call Indians in both a racial and a cultural sense) are a small minority. The National Indian Council (Consejo Indígena Nacional) counts 700,000, 2.3 percent of the national population, and claims to have organized 80 percent of them; it is significant that the council was founded only in 1982, indicating both the status of Indians as a minority and the difficulty of organizing such a dispersed group. The Office of the National Procurator reports that there are more than 1,200 indigenous communities, representing 81 different language groups, and calculates a population of 500,000, 1.5 percent of the nation's population and 4.3 percent of its rural population. There are indigenous

The poor in Bogotá, a shanty home near a mountain (Photo by Harvey F. Kline.)

communities in 190 municipalities in 27 departments, but only 7 municipalities have more than 10,000 Indians. The largest numbers are in the departments of Cauca (with 29 percent of the total Indian population), Guajira (with 19 percent), Nariño (with 9 percent), Chocó (with 5 percent), Cordoba (with 4 percent), Vaupeés and Putumayo (with 3.5 percent each), and Vichada and Guainía (with 3 percent each). The departments in which Indians make up the highest percentage of the population are Vichada and Guainía (more than 80 percent), Vaupeés (65 percent), and Amazonas (32 percent). The largest Indian language group in the country is the Páez, located in Cauca, which makes up 21 percent of the total Indian population. Next in size are the Wayuú of Guajira (18 percent), the Embera of Chocó, Antioquia, and Caldas (9 percent), and the Pasto of Nariño (8 percent). The rest of the Indian population is distributed among 77 language groups, 61 of which represent less than 1 percent of the native population of Colombia.

Most of Colombia's indigenous population (83.5 percent) lives on reservations. Of the 334 reservations, 67 were established before the first agrarian reform law in

1961. These old reservations contain 35 percent of the Indian population, and they are characterized by small landholdings, depletion of the soil, and colonization by non-Indians. The remaining 267 reservations were set up as an aspect of agrarian reform, three-quarters of them in the Amazon and on the Pacific Coast. Some of them still suffer from incomplete boundary marking, insufficient land, and colonization. On the Pacific Coast, in particular, Indians are being forced off their lands by forestry and mining interests, and the production of salt and coal on the La Guajira peninsula has caused sufficient ecological damage to the Wayuú reservation to call for government compensation. The Embera-Waunana Regional Indigenous Organization has recently described its region as 80 percent black, 10 percent Indian, 10 percent mixed; 79.7 percent lacking the basic necessities of life; truancy in the few high schools that exist; an illiteracy rate of 40 percent; an infant mortality rate of 191 per 1,000; and 56 percent of families with monthly income below the government-mandated minimum.[13] The Colombian Institute of Agrarian Reform (Instituto Colombiano de la Reforma Agraria— INCORA) has identified forty-five reservations with shortages of land amounting to some 154,000 hectares and urges socioeconomic studies of some 100 additional indigenous communities that still do not have legal title to their lands. As the Columbus Quincentenary approached in 1992, the government made a special effort to create new Indian reservations. From 1990 to 1992, sixty-seven new reservations were established, granting 852,000 hectares to 66,000 Indians.[14]

These efforts respond to the issue that the native peoples of Colombia have long considered most pressing—the restoration of their traditional tribal lands. A regional indigenous organization was established in the Cauca area in the early 1970s with the objectives of reestablishing Indian reservations, increasing the authority of their local governments, and reaffirming the autonomy of their regions. When the leaders of this Regional Indigenous Council of the Cauca (Consejo Regional Indígena del Cauca, CRIC) were jailed by the local authorities or assassinated by thugs hired by large landowners, members retaliated by joining various guerrilla groups. In 1984 an Indian guerrilla group was formed: the Quintín Lame Armed Movement (Movimiento Armado Quintín Lame), which until the 1990 truce averaged between 100 and 300 members.[15] At least in part because of the demands of indigenous groups, Indians were assigned two seats in the 1991 Constituent Assembly, and the new constitution gave them two seats in the Senate.

The constitution designated no such special seats for blacks, perhaps reflecting the fact that solidarity among blacks has been difficult to achieve. In contrast to the blacks of Brazil or Cuba, Colombia's blacks have preserved little of their African heritage. As Wade points out, "The very structure of the black category and its relationship to the nonblack world is an obstacle. The boundaries of the category at the national level . . . are fuzzy and shifting; opportunities for escape from blackness exist and are made the most of by some blacks, and whatever the personal motives involved, these strategies are frequently understood as a rejection of blackness by some blacks."[16] Just before the signing of the constitution in 1991, the 220 participants in the Fifth Afro-American Encounter in Quibdó made three demands: that Afro-Americans be recognized as a cultural group, that Afro-American territories be given the same status as indigenous ones, and that social justice be established for Colombia's 3.5 million Afro-Americans.[17] Rather than these demands being considered by the Constituent Assembly and incorporated into the new constitution as similar Indian demands had been, the matter was left for the consideration of Congress. In 1993 Congress assigned two seats in the Chamber to the black communities.

Gender

Women make up an increasing proportion of the economically active population (estimated at 43 percent of the workforce in 1989, compared with 38 percent in 1980, 26 percent in 1973, and 19 percent in 1951).[18] Work outside the home has long been the tradition for peasant women and those of the urban lower classes, for whom one income per family is simply not enough. Likewise, upper-class women have long participated in economic activities, leaving child care and housework to hired women from the lower class. University-level education is increasingly a possibility for women. Of women holding employment, 19.7 percent had a university education in 1990 compared with 15.8 in 1984, 14.7 percent in 1980, and 11.6 percent in 1976.[19] The percentage of public education students who are women has increased in recent decades, suggesting that middle-income women as well as men are experiencing mobility through education.

A study conducted in the seven largest cities of Colombia in June 1991 (Table 1.3) showed, however, that women receive lower salaries than men even when educational level is taken into account and are much more likely to be unemployed.[20] A recent study of female prostitutes in Bogotá revealed that, with the exception of those under twenty, who had most often entered the profession

TABLE 1.3 Income Differences by Gender in the Seven Largest Cities of Colombia, June 1991

Income	Men (%)	Women (%)
None	1.6	3.3
Less than 1 minimum salary	24.3	44.5
1–2 minimum salaries	37.7	30.1
2–3 minimum salaries	14.3	10.6
3–4 minimum salaries	4.1	2.5
4–5 minimum salaries	2.8	1.4
More than 5 minimum salaries	7.0	2.5
No information	8.2	5.1

SOURCE: "Indicadores sociales," *Coyuntura Social* 6 (June 1992):59.

because of violence in the home, the major reasons for entering prostitution were lack of income, lack of skill, and lack of other employment opportunities.[21]

Colombian leaders since independence, including Simón Bolívar, have stressed the role of women in the family and the home. During the federal period (1863–1885) women did receive the right to vote in the province of Veélez, but attempts to make that right national failed in 1886, 1936, 1944, and 1946. Women were granted the legal capacity to administer their property in 1932, access to higher education in 1933, and the right to hold nonelected public office in 1936.[22] They received the vote only in 1954, and then by decree of the one military dictator of this century, Gustavo Rojas Pinilla, whose constituent assembly had included two women. Since Rojas permitted no elections, however, women did not vote until the plebiscite for the 1957 constitutional amendment, Article 1 of which said, "Women will have the same political rights as men." Women still vote less often than men and seldom hold political office. Between 1958 and 1972, only 2.1 percent of senators, 4.2 percent of the Chamber members, 7.4 percent of the members of the departmental assemblies, and 6.4 percent of the members of municipal councils were women.[23] In 1991 the corresponding figures were 1 percent of the senators, 5.2 percent of Chamber members, and 2.5 percent of members of municipal councils.[24]

Most of the changes benefiting women have come from presidential initiatives. In 1974, for example, President Alfonso López Michelsen fulfilled his campaign promises to women by abolishing *potestad marital* (the husband's rights over the wife and children). In 1990 President César Gaviria created a Council for Youth, Women, and the Family charged with improving life for those groups, but he appointed a man to head it. In 1991 paid maternity benefits were extended from eight to twelve weeks for women covered by social security.[25] Only 42 percent of the employed women in the four major cities of Colombia (Bogotá, Medellín, Cali, Barranquilla) in 1988 were in jobs that might be covered by social security.[26]

The new constitution of 1991 seemed to give new opportunities to women but only 4 were elected to the 74-member Constituent Assembly. In the proportional-representation election of its members, only 8 of the 119 lists were headed by women. Two notable cases were the all-feminist list headed by Rosa Turizo, prosecutor of the Superior Court of Medellín, and the list presented by nongovernmental organizations and headed by Helena Páez, former minister of labor and adviser to Gaviria's Council for Youth, Women, and the Family. Neither list was elected. Many women supported the Alianza Democrática M-19, and two of the four women elected were from that list. The other two were a Liberal and a leader of the Central Workers' Union elected by the Unión Patriótica. Feminist groups were active in presenting proposals to the Constituent Assembly, among them incorporating into the constitution the UN's statements on women's rights. Although some of these were eventually included, only time will tell if the formal stipulations will be translated into practice.[27]

Women can occasionally reach the top in politics. One example is Noemí Sanín Posada, minister of foreign relations during the government of César Gaviria. Coming from a traditional Antioquian family, she studied law at the Jesuit Universidad Javeriana. Her professional career began in earnest when, having refused four vice ministries and a position as presidential adviser in the government of Belisario Betancur (1982–1986), she accepted an appointment as minister of communication in 1984. During the presidency of Virgilio Barco (1986–1990) Sanín worked in the private sector; when Gaviria became president he named her ambassador to Venezuela, one of Colombia's top three ambassadorial posts.[28] Such exceptions tend to prove the rule that the public arena is dominated by men.

Social Class

In broad terms (although there are regional differences), the great division in Colombia, as in many other places in Latin America, is between a working class that performs manual labor and a professional class. Anecdotal evidence abounds concerning what *gente decente* ("decent people," as people in the professional class call themselves) should not do: carry their own groceries, wash their own clothes, clean their own houses, repair their own cars, and so on. People in the higher-income levels of the working class may actually have more food and better diets than people of similar incomes in the professional class, since the latter have to spend a greater proportion of their income on hired help and on symbols of their prestige—automobiles, clothing, and other consumer goods.

Clearly one's class depends on education, and some sons and daughters of the working class use education to improve their circumstances. Yet in many cases such mobility is not possible. Even free public education for low-income families has a cost in terms of lost income when the children are in school rather than at work. These families need the wages, however meager, of their children. In addition, public education is insufficient in coverage and sometimes poor in quality. A study of 1990 test results of high school graduates who planned to go on to college showed that 25 percent of the private high schools had average student scores significantly above the national average compared with 11 percent of the public high schools. At the other extreme, 41 percent of the private high schools had average student scores below the national average while a full 50 percent of the public high schools had such low scores.

The same study indicated differences among the major cities of Colombia. Bogotá had 35 percent of its high schools above average and 26 percent below average, Medellín 20 and 57 percent respectively; Cali 31 and 28; Barranquilla 12 and 69; and Bucaramanga 36 and 26.[29] Since educational opportunity varies with income, which—in turn—varies with race, these figures indicate that nonwhite Colombians, even in the major cities, have less opportunity than whites. The test scores from Barranquilla are particularly illustrative of this, and the results in that

Supplementing the family income by selling newspapers in the north of Bogotá (Photo by Harvey F. Kline.)

coastal city of black heritage would no doubt be even more lopsided if data were available to differentiate the private from the public high schools. Finally, at the public university level, social mobility prospects are sometimes frustrated by political activities that lead to the closing of the universities. Since the students of those institutions come particularly from public secondary education, the result is that the class and racial bias is aggravated.

There is further stratification within the two large classes. The ideal member of the segment of the upper class called the "oligarchy" has very high income, is of pure Spanish background and even from one of the traditional families (those who have surnames that indicate "pedigree"), has received university education abroad or at one of the prestigious private Colombian universities, and belongs to an exclusive private club. This oligarchy is said to exercise undue political power, although no rigorous study has ever shown this to be the case.[30]

Within the working class there is stratification along income lines, with the top levels having well-paid unionized jobs and the lowest level, the so-called *marginales,* depending for their income on petty commercial activities (selling candy, gum, cigarettes, and the like on the streets), crime, or scavenging. The great majority of members of this marginal economic group are not delinquents; rather, they are the losers in an economic system in which funding of social programs has been declining. In mid-1992 the Bogatá think tank FEDESARROLLO reported that the proportion of the national budget allocated to social programs had declined from 43 percent in 1984 to 34 percent in 1990 when by international standards it should have remained at more than 40 percent.[31] Thus, whereas it may be reasonable for working-class people with higher incomes to strive for mobility through education for their children, it is simply not a possibility for the very poorest.

Middle-income people with professional occupations—doctors, lawyers, government bureaucrats, and employees in private businesses—make up perhaps 30 percent of the population. Their status is ambiguous and their income, with the rapid inflation of recent years, increasingly tenuous. Some Colombian sociologists argue that this group is not a "class" because its members' aspirations are the same as those of wealthier professionals—consumer goods, prestige symbols, good education for their children. They most commonly send their children to private primary and secondary educational institutions, if possible to the most prestigious—and presumably best—so that they will have access to the most exclusive private universities. The wage earners of this middle-income group feel the effects of inflation much more than their more affluent colleagues, however, and may be developing a common identity. They tended to support the New Liberalism of Luis Carlos Galán, for example. Perhaps someday they will even form middle-class interest groups and political parties.

Colombians take great pride in their culture, often referring to Bogotá as the Athens of South America and arguing that the quality of the Spanish spoken there is the best in Latin America. They point to the Nobel Laureate Gabriel García Márquez and the artist Fernando Botero. In their interests and in the contents of their homes there is little to distinguish upper-class Colombians from their counterparts in the United States and western Europe. The working class, in contrast, is distinguished both from the upper class and regionally by food habits, dress, and leisure pursuits. The local beverages include *aguardiente* (an anise-flavored sugar-cane liquor) in the Andes, white rum in the Caribbean coastal area, and the excellent (and comparatively inexpensive) Colombian beer throughout the country. Regional food variations include *ajicaco* (a stew made of chicken, beef, potatoes, plantains, corn, and manioc) in the Bogotá region, *frijoles* and *chicharrones* (beans and pork rinds) in Medellín, and *arroz con coco* (rice cooked with coconut) on the coast. Whereas the urban poor often aspire to dress as upper-class people do, the rural poor still dress in ways traditional to their regions. In Antioquia the peasant still arrives in Medellín with his machete over one shoulder and his *carriel* (a kind of pocketbook for men traditionally made of cowhide with the hair left on it) over the other. In the Caribbean coastal region one can still see the intricately patterned sombreros made of yellow and black straw. In the higher Andes (Cundinamarca and Boyacá, for example), a common outer garment is still the ruana. The music of the poor varies by region as well, including such dances as the salsa, the cumbia, and the *vallenato*.

Modernization

Colombia has recently seen both extremely rapid population growth and an increase in the percentage of people living in urban settings. The population grew from 11.5 million in 1951 to 17.5 million in 1964, 22.5 million in 1973, 27.3 million in 1980, and 29 million in 1986. The estimate for 1994 was 35 million. These figures indicate growth rates of 3.2 percent per annum between 1951 and 1964, 2.7 percent between 1964 and 1973, and 1.6 percent between 1973 and 1985. At the same time, the urban population (defined by the Colombian government as the population of settlements of more than 5,000) had increased from 38.9 percent in 1951 to 66.6 percent in 1986. Colombia has always been a country of many large cities, in contrast to the many Latin American countries in which one city dominates the nation.

Of the various indicators of the change in education, health, and quality of life (Table 1.4), perhaps most important is the decline of illiteracy from nearly 38 percent in 1950 to 11 percent in 1985. This reflects the growth of educational opportunities in the country (Table 1.5). At all levels education grew more rapidly than the population, with primary education increasing by 11 and 9 percent per year in the 1960s and 1970s respectively, secondary education by 19 and 24 percent in the

TABLE 1.4   Indicators of Change in Colombia, 1950 and 1985

Characteristic	*1950*	*1985*
Number of telephones per 1,000 inhabitants	6.19	90.58
Electricity generated (watts per capita)	20	942
Percentage of population in		
Primary education	7.1	14.2
Secondary education	0.6	7.8
Postsecondary education	0.0009	0.015
Illiteracy rate (per 1,000)	37.7	11.0
Number of inhabitants per physician	3,310	1,200
Infant mortality rate (deaths per 1,000)	163	40

SOURCE: *El Espectador* (Bogotá), April 13, 1986.

TABLE 1.5   School Enrollment in Colombia (in thousands), 1940–1988

Year	Primary	Secondary	Postsecondary
1940	606.0	61.7	3.0
1950	808.5	79.6	10.6
1960	1,690.4	229.7	22.7
1970	3,286.1	791.8	92.1
1980	3,597.4	1,433.6	303.1
1988	4,044.2	2,076.5	434.6

SOURCE: María Teresa Forero de Saade, Leonardo Cañón Ortegón, and Javier Armando Pineda Duque (eds.), *Mujer trabajadora: Nuevo compromiso social* (Bogotá: Instituto de Estudios Sociales Juan Pablo II, 1991), 51.

same two decades, and postsecondary education by 25 percent in the 1950s, 30 percent in the 1970s, and 23 percent in the 1980s.

The decline in the population growth rate, once one of the highest in the world, is attributed to a government-sponsored family planning program and to the effects of urbanization. Rural poor people not only were uneducated in birth control methods but also saw a certain logic in large families—more children to help in the fields and to serve as a form of "social security" for later years. These same people, having moved to the cities, no longer needed the workforce or the social security provided by a large family. Of course, there was a time lag before behavioral patterns actually changed. Nevertheless, the population is still growing very rapidly. Whereas Colombia was doubling its population every 22.5 years during the 1951–1964 period, with the lower growth rate doubling will now occur in 45 years; 480,000 Colombians are still being born each year.

The move to the cities has had several causes. Some migrants have been forced out of the countryside by political violence and the mechanization of agriculture. Others have been drawn to the cities by the hope of a better life—better housing, jobs, schools for their children, the excitement of living where things are happening. Urban jobs, however, have not kept pace with population growth. In 1985, at the height of a recession, 14 percent of the urban population was officially unemployed, and many more had simply quit looking for jobs. Many unemployed Colombians enter the so-called informal sector, in which they live a day-to-day existence as extremely small-scale merchants, restaurateurs, or service-sector operatives.

Many Colombians believe that poverty leads to lawlessness—that unemployed adults in the cities turn to robbery in order to feed their children. (This of course implies that only through economic growth can lawlessness be curtailed.)

In 1983 the national police, in their magazine *Criminalidad,* reported alarming crime statistics: a homicide every sixty minutes, an attack every hour, a personal-injury crime every twelve minutes, seventeen frauds every day, and eight crimes of kidnapping or of a sexual nature every twenty-four hours. About 90 percent of the crimes went unreported. At about the same time the minister of justice, Rodrigo Lara, reported that there were only 42 guilty verdicts in 2,500 murder trials. The courts were overloaded, and so were the prisons.[32] Conditions have worsened in the years since these 1983 reports. During the 1980s homicide became the leading cause of death in Colombia; in 1990 there were 24,267 murders, 75.95 per 100,000 inhabitants, about 18 percent of which were political. In the same year 1,282 kidnappings were reported to the authorities, and that number rose in the following two years.[33]

Conclusion

From the above it is clear that life in Colombia varies dramatically by region, race, gender, income, and social class. Air transport, internal migration, radio and television, and other aspects of modernization are leading to a more unified nation, but sharp social distinctions remain.

Notes

1. *Atlas básico de Colombia* (Bogotá: Instituto Geográfico "Agustín Codazzi," 1980), 6.

2. James J. Parsons, *Antioqueño Colonization in Western Colombia* (Berkeley: University of California Press, 1968), 62–63.

3. This important point was brought to my attention by Colombian sociologist Armando Borrero Mansilla in July 1992.

4. Figures from the Departamento Administrativo Nacional de Estadística, quoted in *El Mundo* (Medellín), November 21, 1983.

5. Calculated from data presented in Julio Silva Colmenares, *Los verdaderos dueños del país* (Bogotá: Fondo Editorial Suramérica, 1977), 233.

6. In the 1960s, one social scientist from the United States arrived in Bogotá with a plan to measure race for his study. The idea was to match one of a series of cards with different skin tones to the person being interviewed. However, since he realized that the amount of time in the sun would affect the match, the instructions were going to be to have the interviewer make the identification at an area not affected by sunlight—at the underarm. This plan was abandoned when the Colombian interviewers told the gringo social scientist that it simply would not work. I first heard this story soon after it took place. I have now verified it through a Confidential Interview, Colombian Sociologist, February 1, 1993. This individual was one of the interviewers who took part in the study.

7. Peter Wade, *Blackness and Race Mixture: The Dynamics of Racial Identity in Colombia* (Baltimore: Johns Hopkins University Press, 1993), 25.

8. Wade, *Blackness and Race Mixture,* 20.

9. Ibid., 14–15.

10. Ibid., 18.

11. *El Espectador* (Bogotá), August 16, 1992.

12. Wade, *Blackness and Race Mixture,* 295.

13. *El Espectador* (Bogotá), March 29, 1992.

14. Procuraduría General de la Nación, *II informe sobre derechos humanos* (Bogotá: n.p., 1993), 66–72.

15. Comisión de Superación de la Violencia, *Pacificar la paz: Lo que no se ha negociado en los acuerdos de paz* (Bogotá: Instituto de Estudios Políticos y Relaciones Internacionales de la Universidad Nacional, 1992), 104–105.

16. Wade, *Blackness and Race Mixture,* 325–326.

17. *El Espectador* (Bogotá), June 18, 1991.

18. Figures from the Departamento Administrativo Nacional de Estadística, quoted in Mariía Teresa Forero de Saade, Leonardo Cañón Ortegón, and Javier Armando Pineda Duque (eds.), *Mujer trabajadora: Nuevo compromiso social* (Bogotá: Instituto de Estudios Sociales Juan Pablo II, 1991), 49.

19. Forero de Saade, Cañón Ortegón, and Pineda Duque, *Mujer trabajadora,* 53.

20. "Indicadores sociales," *Coyuntura Social* 6 (June 1992):57.

21. "Profile: Prostitutes in Bogotá," *Hemisphere* 5 (Fall 1992):31.

22. Martha I. Morgan, "Constitution Making in a Time of Cholera: Women and the 1991 Colombian Constitution," *Yale Journal of Law and Feminism* 4 (1992):359–361.

23. Shirley Harkness and Patricia Pinzón de Lewin, "Women, the Vote, and the Party in the Politics of the Colombian National Front," *Journal of Interamerican Studies and World Affairs* 17 (1975):443.

24. Morgan, "Constitution Making," 363.

25. Ibid., 362–363.

26. Forero de Saade, Cañón Ortegón, and Pineda Duque, *Mujer trabajadora,* 61.

27. Morgan, "Constitution Making," 373.

28. *Semana,* May 11, 1993.

29. "Indicadores sociales," 25–26.

30. Colombian social scientists (especially those of the left) constantly refer to the oligarchy. For a North American's attempt to show empirically that it does not exist, see James J. Payne, "The Oligarchy Muddle," *World Politics* 20 (1968):439–453.

31. "Indicadores sociales," 7.

32. *El Espectador* (Bogotá), June 5, 1983.

33. "Indicadores sociales," 46, 48.

2

COLOMBIA FROM
PREHISTORY TO 1930

COLOMBIA HAD FEWER INDIANS than Mexico, Guatemala, Bolivia, or Peru at the time, perhaps three to four million, when the Spanish reached it in about 1530. Some, such as the Caribs and Arawaks, were warlike hunters and fishers. Many had developed agriculture and produced goldwork that attracted the conquerors. Among these were the Calima (Valle del Cauca), the San Agustín (Huila), the Tumaco (Nariño), the Quimbaya (Caldas, Risaralda, Quindío), the Tairona (Sierra Nevada de Santa Marta), and the Guane (southern Santander). By far the most complex Indian society of the time was the Chibcha (or Muisca) of the highlands of what are today Cundinamarca and Boyacá. The Chibchas had established densely settled agricultural communities and developed a relatively complex sociopolitical organization.[1] Other complex Indian societies had already disappeared; the civilization in the valley of San Agustín, for example, was represented only by its temples and statues.

Empires and large cities never existed in prehistoric Colombia, nor were there any forts or major irrigation works or elaborate tombs. Rather, there were small chiefdoms or at most incipient states scattered throughout the mountains and along the coasts. Instead of monuments, the sparse remains tend to be of the simple way of life of forest dwellers, highland farmers, fishermen, and villagers.[2]

Early gatherers were in present-day Colombia perhaps by 11,000 B.C. and early hunters by about 8000 B.C. About 3000 B.C. there appeared on the Caribbean seaboard of Colombia a well-defined pattern of life, that of the shell-mound dwellers. For the next 2,000 or more years these peoples spread over the seashores and lagoons and established a way of life characteristic of the so-called Archaic or pre-Formative stage in the Americas. Their shell-fishing sites are the earliest-known dated archaeological horizon in Colombia. The principal site and the one that has yielded the earliest radiocarbon dates is the Puerto Hormiga shell-mound, at the mouth of the Canal del Dique near Cartagena. Until a recent discovery in the Amazon area of Brazil, pottery found at Puerto Hormiga was the earliest in the Americas.

The move of the population inland came with the development of agricultural crops. The first of these was manioc (yuca), but it was the introduction of corn that seems to have allowed a growing population to settle the mountain flanks, until then sparsely populated by hunters. Scattered farms became the norm. According to Gerardo Reichel-Dolmatoff,

> Adaptation to the individual micro-environments brought about diversification and the growth of local cultures which, although sometimes they occupied neighboring valleys, differed widely in their scope and content. There were no "cotraditions" nor "horizon-styles" comparable with those found in the Central Andes, but a marked diversity due to geographic and cultural isolation, and due to different ways of coping with the local environment.[3]

Mesoamerican influences in Colombia date from as early as 1200 B.C., when such elements as the jaguar cult, corn cultivation, burial mounds, and monolithic sarcophagi were introduced by sporadic settlers from the Pacific coast.

By about 500 B.C., Mesoamerican influence was again making itself felt in the southern Pacific lowlands, between the mouth of the San Juan River and the off-shore island of Tumaco, and this influence moved inland four major groups developed in the western part of what is today Colombia: San Agustín, Tierradentro, Calima, and Quimbaya. Although they differed from one another in many respects, they were all based on intensive corn farming and sedentary life. Fields with ridges and furrows were common. A well-defined social order is suggested by discriminative treatment of the dead. Their pottery had many characteristics in common, and stone carvings were found in all four areas. Gold and copper metallurgy suggests links among them.[4] Hilltops were leveled for houses and burial mounds, slopes terraced for fields, and canals, drainage ditches, and roadways built. The major constructions, including the stone carvings and burial mounds, began about the time of Christ.[5]

The two periods of Mesoamerican influence gave rise to a new culture pattern in which seed agriculture laid the foundation for sedentary village life and, although shifting agriculture continued, settlements were far more permanent than before. The consequent concentration of an increasing population led to social stratification, craft specialization, high technological development, and trade. Wider political cohesion was achieved only when a group of neighboring valleys became united under a local chief.[6]

In the Sinú Valley, mound-builders and goldsmiths were still flourishing when the first Spanish expeditions arrived; here the chieftains of three tribal confederations were brothers who combined political authority with priestly functions. In the rain-forest region of the San Juan River there were small agricultural settlements on the banks of the main river and some of its tributaries. The mountains and valleys of Antioquia were densely populated by Indians who had formed large confederations under local chieftains. The fertile, well-watered soils and the rich gold mines, together with the region's strategic location as a contact area, provided a favorable context for this development. Somewhere in the desolate valley of Arbi, reconnoitering Spanish troops found "very large ancient buildings, all in ruins, and roads of dressed stone, made by human hands, larger than those of Cuzco, and cabins in the manner of store houses." Caribs from the Guianas and the Venezuelan coast had established themselves in the Colombian lowlands and conquered the small villages there and in the foothills of the interior.[7]

The Tairona of the Sierra Nevada foothills, perhaps numbering as many as 700,000, lived in large nucleated villages, often located strategically for easy defense. Their principal towns were Bonda and Pocigueica, both inhabited by thousands, and for some of the valleys the chronicles mention hundreds and even thousands of houses. Warfare was important, but as a rule every village conducted its own, rarely joining forces with others. It took the Spanish the better part of a century to subdue the Tairona, who, after periods of uneasy peace, rebelled again and again against the invaders. The last great rebellion occurred in 1599 and was suppressed in 1600 after three months of fierce battles in which all resistance was broken and the tribe apparently ceased to exist as a unit.[8]

The Chibcha or Muisca of the bleak plateaus of Cundinamarca and Boyacá were organized into two loose federations, one controlling the southern highlands, centered around Bogotá, and the other in the region of Tunja. They had domesticated a large number of highland crops and built terraces for their cultivation, and they exchanged salt, emeralds, and cotton cloth for gold and other luxury articles. In terms of political cohesion, social structure, religious complexity, and economic efficiency, Chibcha society contrasted sharply with its neighbors.[9]

The indigenous population declined rapidly after the arrival of the Spanish under the pressure of warfare, disease, miscegenation, and abortion (apparently a choice of women who did not wish to raise children in a situation of servitude or ones who would be ostracized because of miscegenation). By the beginning of the seventeenth century the population had declined to some 600,000 and by 1789 to 136,753.[10]

The Spanish Colony

The first Spaniard to reach the shores of Colombia was Alfonso de Ojeda, who explored the Guajira coast in 1500. In 1509 Ojeda founded a settlement near Cartagena, but it did not last. The first permanent settlements were Cartagena (1533) and Santa Marta (1535).

The city of Santafé de Bogotá was founded in 1538 by Gonzalo Jiménez de Queseda. Two other conquerors independently reached the city the following year: Sebastián de Belalcázar, from Ecuador, and Nikolaus Federmann, from Venezuela. In 1549 an *audiencia* (high court of justice) was established in the city and in 1563 a captaincy general. The captaincy general was formally part of the viceroyalty of Peru, centered in the far-off city of Lima. Distance made it difficult for the viceroy to maintain effective control over the situation in Bogotá. Further, the captain general in Bogotá had great difficulty in maintaining control over the leaders in the six parts of the captaincy general: Cartagena, Santa Marta, Riohacha, Antioquia, Popayán, and Panamá. Indeed, it has been argued that the Catholic church was more effective than the government.[11]

The captaincy general was neither a backwater of Spanish colonization nor a principal center like Lima or Mexico. Cartagena developed into a major port through which all trade with South America (including the silver of Peru) was expected to flow. A small number of Spanish colonizers had come to Colombia for its natural riches, especially gold and emeralds. The *encomienda* (a system through which the Spanish crown granted Indians to landowners, who were to care for and Christianize them in return for their work) was limited by the scarcity of settled and peaceful Indians to the highlands, especially the Chibcha area. African slaves were brought to the Caribbean coast region and the gold-mining areas of Antioquia and Chocó. Miscegenation began throughout the captaincy general. In 1739 Bogotá became the capital of the new viceroyalty of Nueva Granada (including today's countries of Colombia, Panama, Venezuela, and Ecuador).

Independence and Gran Colombia

One of the cities of Colombia, Cartagena, declared its independence in May 1810, before anyone had made such a statement for the viceroyalty as a whole. After Bogotá declared its independence on July 20, 1810, the country entered a period that came to be called "the foolish fatherland" (*patria boba*). Parts of the country never declared independence (Popayán, Panamá, Santa Marta), and those parts that did proved unable to cooperate with each other. It is not surprising under the circumstances that the Spanish were able to reconquer the territory in 1815–1816. Definitive independence for Colombia came in August 1819 with the battle of Boyacá, in which the Spanish were defeated by patriot forces led by the Venezuelan Simón Bolívar after a lightning trip up the mountains from the Orinoco region. Thus Colombia's independence came the second time around, and the new leader was a Venezuelan who already recognized its regional differences.

In 1821, through the Constitution of Cúcuta, a government was set up for the entire former viceroyalty, to be called Gran Colombia. Bolívar continued south to fight for the independence of Ecuador (1822) and Peru and Bolivia (1824), leaving behind his vice president, the Colombian Francisco de Paula Santander, to govern the new nation. Yet—given already existing regional identities and problems of transportation—the experiment was doomed from the start. In 1827 Bolívar returned to Bogotá to find that unity was breaking down. He tried to impose a virtual constitutional monarchy only to meet with rejection of Venezuelans, military people, and strong government. He managed to establish a dictatorship without constitutional sanction in 1828 and survived an assassination attempt, but Gran Colombia was breaking up nevertheless. Bolívar resigned in March 1830 and died in December of the same year.

The failure of Gran Colombia revealed a commitment on the part of the Colombian elite to civilian rule that was to limit military dictatorships to only one in the nineteenth century and one in the twentieth, in contrast to the experience of most other countries of Latin America. Three explanations for this anomaly have been offered: that the military establishment that brought independence was not Colombian but mostly Venezuelan, that the civilian elite in Colombia, unlike that in other countries, had not been destroyed by the wars of independence, and that the military men who brought independence were not only Venezuelan but often men of color and therefore unacceptable to the white *gente decente* of Bogotá.[12] For these reasons and others, a preference for "democracy" accompanied by weak government developed. The army and the police force were kept small and weak to exclude them from politics, and as a consequence, law enforcement, especially in the rural areas of the country, was left in private hands.

The First Century of Colombian Independence

After the failure of the Gran Colombia experiment, what we now call Colombia was on its own as an independent country. Factions soon developed and the political parties that have dominated national life began to emerge.

Political Cleavages

Politics in the early years of the country were personalistic (dominated by the strong personalities of individual leaders) and volatile. The writing of the constitution was pursued with more concern for contemporary European ideologies than for national reality. Regionalism continued to be important; the viceroyalty had never integrated the country, and neither had the independence wars. There were new conflicts between leaders who had participated in the wars of independence and those who had not. The country was poor and only sparsely settled (the first census, in 1851, showed a population of only 2.25 million). Most people lived in quasi-feudal situations known as *patrias chicas* as the clients of large landowners (patrons), and the cities were very small. The government was weak. In the rural areas the owners of large estates were, in effect, the government. They administered justice and incarcerated peasants who misbehaved. Although there were some economic benefits for groups that obtained control of the national government, the bureaucratic positions and tax collections were not sufficient to satisfy them.[13]

The first civil war took place between 1838 and 1842. It began with what appeared to be a trivial event—the abolition of small monasteries in Nariño—but took on great importance in a society with deep-rooted religious values, regional religious groups that had great difficulty in surviving, and a powerful Catholic church. Landowners also were searching for an excuse for a fight, albeit over different issues (e.g., land tenure and loans). The conflict was therefore long and widespread, and it established violence as sometimes a legitimate recourse.

The personalist nature of politics began to abate between 1845 and 1848, when representatives of the merchants assumed a larger role at the invitation of government itself. By 1849 there was an alternative form of social organization to that of the colonial latifundia—mercantile capital. Governments up to this point had been protectionist in their tariff policies, encouraging artisan development. By 1846 there were numerous urban artisan groups promoted by merchants connected with them and by a group of young lawyers. These groups, which came to be called "democratic societies," grew rapidly and ceased to be limited to artisans. In competition with this type of political organization, the Jesuits founded "popular" or "Catholic" societies. By 1850 the major cities had many of both kinds of society. The social basis was thus laid for the creation of political parties. On one side were the traditional *latifundistas* in alliance with the Catholic church, on the other the merchants and artisans.

During the term in office of General José Hilario López (1849–1853), who was elected by Congress under considerable pressure from the artisan groups, the merchants were able to implement a series of reforms that destroyed the colonial institutional structure. As Francisco Leal has argued, "In essence, these reforms sought to create economic bases which would substitute for, or at least liberate the merchants from, the political class domination of large landowners whose power base lay in the 'static' social organization inherited from the colonial period."[14] The major reforms included abolition of the tobacco monopoly, which meant free cultivation and commercialization of the crop; a suspension of *censos* (church mortgages) when the state took them over in 1851–1852; the elimination (in 1850) of Indian reservations, making possible commercialization of their land and the freeing of Indian labor; a direct form of taxation (1850–1851) based on a fiscal and administrative decentralization; and the emancipation in 1851 of the 20,000 remaining slaves. It is not surprising that a civil war broke out in 1851 in the west and central regions of the country—regions in which the latifundia depended heavily on slavery.

"Sectarian Democracy"

The two parties—Liberal and Conservative—that came to dominate Colombian politics were established in 1849 and by the end of the López administration had become somewhat organized. Their first programs were very similar. Both parties defended liberty, justice, order, and political and religious tolerance; both were averse to dictatorship and called themselves democratic.[15] The period from 1849 to 1953 can be called the one of sectarian democracy combining of civilian government and parties with violence and civil war. Certain patterns of behavior developed that affect Colombian politics to some extent even today.[16]

Ideological Differences. The two parties soon developed different programs that were at least to a certain degree carried out when each was in power.[17] The Liberals stood for federalism and free trade and were anticlerical. The Conservatives favored unitary government and protectionism and were proclerical. There were notable exceptions to these generalizations, including a Conservative president who was instrumental in the approval of a federalist constitution. Indeed, most of the Conservative party joined President Mariano Ospina Rodríguez in support of the federal constitution of 1858, as "the federal republic, fruit of the spirit of innovation, was generally accepted."[18]

In essence, the ideological difference over time came to be one about the proper role in society of the Catholic church. Indeed, much of the intensity of the political struggles of the nineteenth century stemmed from their religious component. While the Liberals were surely Catholic (and at times made special efforts to demonstrate that they were not antichurch), they opposed clerical activism outside of the religious sphere. Conservatives used their proclerical position to mobilize the masses. As the Colombian historian Germán Colmenares has put it, "There remained only one road that opened access to the masses for the Conservative party. . . . The only Conservative banner that had life and demonstrated resolution and vigor was that which used religious sentiments. *Rojismo* [Liberalism] had no enemy in New Granada that could confront it except Catholicism."[19] A declaration of holy war was extremely clear as early as 1853 when an *Exposición Católica* by the Conservative Rufino Cuervo was read in all the churches of Bogotá and later disseminated throughout the country. The Conservative party was the beneficiary of this exposition.

Whereas Colombians could agree to disagree about the other parts of the party programs, they could not easily accept disagreement about the religious question. As the Colombian sociologist Orlando Fals Borda has argued,

This religious struggle—emotional, bitter, and personal—made social class consciousness secondary and eliminated conflicts based on popular self-identification. Colombian political parties were turned into mere agglomerations of members of the elite and those of the lower classes who shared their inclinations. . . . For this reason, far from being an "element of national unity" and of "social order" as the Constitution says, the Catholic religion has really been a source of conflict and a root of the bitter disunity among Colombians.[20]

This religious aspect of the conflict increased after 1861, when a Liberal government confiscated church lands. It is estimated that the Catholic church owned one-third of the land at the time.

Multiclass Parties. Colombian parties have always been multiclass ones. Both parties have always had both elite and mass sectors, and the division of the elite has never been neat. Although the original elite division was between *latifundistas* (the Conservatives) and merchant capital (the Liberals), the two groups recognized that they had interests in common. The *latifundistas* soon understood the direction of change and hurried to adapt themselves to it and take full advantage of new conditions, even federalism and free trade. Both groups realized that they could put their differences aside when the power of the lower classes seemed to be increasing, as in the 1854 coup of General José María Melo (the century's only military government).[21] Indeed, the dividing line between the two groups was never completely clear; merchants might be *latifundistas* temporarily operating as speculators and usurers, merchants dependent on the incipient foreign trade whose clients were *latifundistas,* or merchants supported by the limited agricultural and artisan commercialization.[22]

Violent Conflict. Political competition was not limited to peaceful means; of the eight civil wars during the nineteenth century, six pitted all (or part) of one party against the other. Through these civil wars the peasant masses "participated" in national politics. Of course, this did not mean that the masses had influence on the elites; most of their participation was required of them by their patrons, and thousands of poor campesinos died.

The longest, cruelest, and most devastating of these violent conflicts between the two parties was the War of the Thousand Days, which began in July 1899 with a Liberal revolt aimed at unseating the Conservative government. Beginning in the department of Santander, the conflict soon spread to other departments. The largest battle was that of Palonegro (near Bucaramanga, Santander) in May 1900, in which 15,000 government troops defeated 14,000 Liberal rebels. After nine months of war "the soil of the fatherland was inundated with blood, thousands of Colombians had died on the battlefields, there was a considerable number of wounded in the hospitals, and the country found itself completely ruined."[23] Yet the war continued until June 1902, and at the end of it the balance sheet included more than 100,000 dead, more with disabling injuries, commerce ruined, communications disrupted, economic production reduced to almost nothing, and a paper peso that was worth less than a gold centavo.[24]

Party Identification. The numerous civil wars and the widespread participation of the campesinos in them led to a rigorous and intense partisan socialization of the masses. Many (if not most) campesino families had their "martyrs"— members killed, disabled, or raped by members of the other political party. While their original party identification was that of their patrons, at some point this identification developed a life of its own. As Eduardo Santa, a Colombian sociologist, has argued, Colombians began to be born "with party identification attached to their umbilical cords."[25] Other cleavages (such as social class and regionalism) became secondary to the party one. Although the elite of either party was often divided in terms of ideology, economic interests, personal loyalties, and even regional allegiances, in the face of a challenge from the other party, factional differences were set aside.

Coalitions. While the masses learned to hate each other and died for their parties, elite party members often entered into bipartisan electoral and governmental

TABLE 2.1   Bipartisan Coalitions in Colombian History, 1845–1949

Year	Name	Participants	Purpose and Stipulations
1854	–	Conservatives	Against dictatorship of José María Melo; two secretaries of state, one from each party
1854	–	Conservatives, Radical Liberals	To elect Manuel María Mallorino vice president
1857	National Party	Parts of both parties	To support candidacy of Tomás Cipriano de Mosquera
1867	–	Conservatives, Radical Liberals	Against the strong Mosquera government
1869	–	Conservatives, Radical Liberals	To elect Mosquera; equal representation in Congress and other public corporations, mutual assent on all political problems
1883–1886	National Party	Conservatives, Independent Liberals	In support of Rafael Núñez and his "regeneration"; a failed attempt to get all factions into the cabinet and do away with old parties
1904–1909	–	Parts of both parties	As part of reconciliation after War of the Thousand Days; two Liberals in cabinet of six
1909–1914	Republican Union	Parts of both parties	Against strong government of Rafael Reyes; after his fall, continued through sharing of cabinet posts

TABLE 2.1   (continued)

Year	Name	Participants	Purpose and Stipulations
1914–1922	–	Parts of both parties	A continuation of the Republican Union without using name; minority representation of Liberals in the cabinet; support of Moderate Conservative presidential candidate through 1918
1930–1932	National Concentration	Parts of both parties	To support Enrique Olaya candidacy; bipartisan cabinet
1946	National Union—Lleras C.	Liberals, Moderate Conservatives	Political conflict over Alfonso López Pumarejo; general instability; three Moderate Conservatives in cabinet
1946–1948; 1948–1949	National Union	Liberals, Moderate Conservatives	In support of candidacy of Mariano Ospina; after election, in response to being a minority president and to the violence, especially after the death of José Eliécer Gaitán; cabinet divided equally, six from each party; "crossover" system in departments, with governors and secretaries of government from different parties

SOURCE: Harvey F. Kline, "The National Front: Historical Perspective and Overview," in R. Albert Berry, Ronald G. Hellman, and Mauricio Solaún (eds.), *Politics of Compromise: Coalition Government in Colombia* (New Brunswick, N.J.: Transaction Books, 1980), 68–69. Reprinted with permission of the publisher.

coalitions (see Table 2.1). These coalitions tended to form when presidents assumed dictatorial powers, when party hegemonies shifted, and, particularly in the current century, when elite-instigated violence was out of control.[26] Indeed, it might be argued that the elites have taken their party identification less seriously than the masses.

The first bipartisan coalition was formed between the Conservatives and a faction of the Liberals called the Gólgotas or Radicals against the dictatorship of Melo. The government of José de Obaldía, the rightful designate, that was formed in Ibagué included two secretaries of state, one from each party, thus demonstrating "parity" for the first time. Later in the same year the Conservatives and the Radical Liberals joined to elect Manuel María Mallarino vice president of the republic.[27] These two approaches—parity and support of a joint candidate—have been common ever since.

Party Government. The preference for civilian, "democratic" government persisted, and "democratic" government meant party government. In the nineteenth century there were only three dictatorships (only one of which was a military one). None lasted more than one and a half years, and all were terminated by partisan opposition. "Democratic" government also meant weak government. The military and national police were viewed as potential opponents of the parties, and a strong constabulary force constructed by one party might well be used against it when the other party came to power. Even civilian bureaucracies were to be kept weak, as there was always the possibility that a strong one would be lost to the opposition party either through revolution or through elections.

Federalism to Centralism. Through the constitutions of 1853, 1858, and 1863, Colombia became one of the most federalist systems in the world. According to the Rionegro Constitution (1863), each of the federated states was sovereign, the central government having control over foreign relations. There were no limits to individual liberties, and each state had its own army. It is said that when Victor Hugo, whom Colombians consider the Constitution's intellectual author, saw the document he remarked, "This must be a country of angels."[28] Given the complete freedom for arms production and traffic, civil wars and violence were rampant. Between 1863 and 1885 there were more than fifty insurrections, as well as forty-two different constitutions in the nine states.[29]

Extreme federalism was abandoned only in 1885, when the Conservatives and the Independent Liberals formed a coalition to support Rafael Núñez. Supporters of the "Regeneration"—as the Núñez government was called—formed a new political organization called the "National Party." By mid-1888 the preponderance of Conservatives within that group was clear, and some of the Independent Liberals drifted back to the Liberal party.[30]

Although the National Party did not last long, the Constitution of 1886, which reversed the earlier federalism, remained in force (albeit significantly amended over time) until 1991. No longer would the national government in Bogotá be weaker than the regional governments. No longer would the president of Colombia be a lesser caudillo than those who ran the states; rather, he would name the governors of the departments. No longer would there be state militias.

Foreign Investment and Imperialism

During most of the nineteenth century, Colombia was not part of any international system; it had no product that could be exported consistently in order to earn foreign exchange. It was only after the 1870s that coffee came to play this role. The coffee merchants who sold the crop to foreign roasters were investing their profits in import-substitution industry, especially in Medellín, as early as the first decade of this century. Foreign capital in the form of loans began to be important in the 1820s, and later foreign interests entered into gold mining. By the 1880s the construction of railroads was the principal form of foreign investment. When the Colombian Senate refused to ratify a treaty with the United States for the construction of a canal in the department of Panamá, the U.S. government of Theodore Roosevelt encouraged a rebellion and prevented Colombian troops from reaching Colón. The United States quickly recognized the new Republic of Panama and signed a treaty for the canal that was even more favorable to it than the one the Senate had rejected.[31] In the years that followed, Colombia became increasingly dependent on the United States. The United Fruit Company (UFCO) bought land on the Caribbean coast and set up "banana enclaves." By the 1920s Colombian troops were assisting in putting down labor-union activities.

This dependency became most apparent during the 1920s in the "Dance of the Millions," when the Colombian government borrowed US$173 million and received another US$25 million in compensation for the loss of Panamá. It has been suggested by both North American and Colombian scholars that the indemnity was contingent upon permission for U.S. petroleum companies to enter the country. Standard Oil of New Jersey was allowed in even before the damages had been paid.[32] Gulf arrived a few years later, and both were awarded long-term concessions.

All of this took place in a period of unusual political calm. After the War of the Thousand Days and the loss of Panamá, a spirit of interparty collaboration materialized that crystallized in the administration of Rafael Reyes (1904–1909). Advancing themes such as "peace and brotherhood" and "less politics and more administration," Reyes, a Conservative, formed a government in which two of the six ministers were Liberals.[33] He introduced a new system of voting for the Congress according to which two-thirds of the seats within an electoral district would go to the party receiving the most votes, the other third going to the losing party.[34] By giving the minority Liberals some representation in government at the national level he hoped to reduce the intensity of their opposition and bring peace. Even after he was forced from power in 1909, coalition governments continued until 1922. At that time the Liberals decided to go their own way, unsuccessfully offering candidates for the presidency for the rest of the decade.

By the late 1920s Colombia had become a much more complex country. Foreign interests were important, and new economic groups had arisen with import-substitution industrialization and the development of a larger financial sector. Popular groups such as unionized workers and landless peasants were becoming restless. With the crisis of the Great Depression, the Liberals, taking advantage of divisions within the ruling conservative party, returned to power for the first time since 1885.

Conclusion

By 1930 Colombia was no longer a "new nation." Its first hundred years had produced a sectarian democracy characterized by civilian government within a weak state and the legitimate use of violence to achieve political goals reinforced when amnesty was granted to the losing side after a civil war. Intensity was conferred on the system by the religious nature of the division between Liberals and Conservatives. All of these choices were logical in their time. The experience of other Latin American countries was showing that armies and police forces tended to usurp civilian power. The granting of amnesty to the losing side after a civil war was sensible both as a precedent for the future (when the winning side might change) and because neither side was likely to have won any civil war overwhelmingly. Finally, the Conservatives' use of religion seemed to be their only rational choice against the Liberals, whose public policies were clearly detrimental to the traditional large landowners and to the church as a temporal power.

These developments did, however, contain the potential for systemic dysfunction. As Alfonso López Michelsen was to point out in 1991, they amounted to a trade-off. Having decided that violence would not originate in the government, Colombia had created a situation in which violence arose from the lack of it, "the absence of discipline, and the propensity to anarchy. . . . The rule has been impunity and, in exceptional cases, excessive punishment. From this, the reason has been the inverse of what is supposed, or that because of the weakness of the State, citizens began taking justice into their own hands." Quoting an unnamed source from forty years before, López continued, "We are proud, both among ourselves and before outsiders, of being a model democracy, but the fact that a political dictatorship does not exist impedes us from recognizing the dominion of terror, of abuse, and of contempt for the law, in which all of the identical phenomena of a dictatorship are met, while we insist that we are avoiding them."[35] The partisan conflicts in Colombia since 1930 have been over which elements of the traditions of sectarian democracy should be maintained and which abandoned.

Notes

1. *Atlas básico de Colombia,* 15.

2. Gerardo Reichel-Dolmatoff, *Ancient Peoples and Places: Colombia* (New York: Praeger, 1965), 17.

3. Ibid., 82.

4. Ibid., 109–110.

5. Robert A. Feldman and Michael E. Moseley, "The Northern Andes," in Jesse D. Jennings (ed.), *Ancient South Americans* (San Francisco: W. H. Freeman, 1983), 169.

6. Reichel-Dolmatoff, *Ancient Peoples and Places,* 115.

7. Ibid., 128, 130, 136.

8. Ibid., 138–139.

9. Ibid., 158–161.

10. *El Espectador* (Bogotá), September 27, 1992.

11. John Edwin Fagg, *Latin America: A General History* (New York: Macmillan, 1963), 361.

12. J. Mark Ruhl, "Civil-Military Relations in Colombia: A Societal Explanation," *Journal of Interamerican Studies and World Affairs* 23 (1981):133.

13. The rest of this section is based on Francisco Leal Buitrago, "Social Classes, International Trade, and Foreign Capital in Colombia: An Attempt at Historical Interpretation of the Formation of the State, 1819–1935" (Ph.D. diss., University of Wisconsin, 1974), 65–81.

14. Ibid., 81.

15. Eduardo Santa, *Sociología política de Colombia* (Bogotá: Ediciones Tercer Mundo, 1964), 44–48.

16. Harvey F. Kline, "From Rural to Urban Society: The Transformation of Colombian Democracy," in Donald L. Herman (ed.), *Democracy in Latin America: Colombia and Venezuela* (New York: Praeger, 1988), 18–20.

17. Two North Americans who have argued that ideology has never been very important in Colombian politics are Vernon Lee Fluharty, *Dance of the Millions: Military Rule and Societal Revolution in Colombia 1930–1956*, 2nd edn. (Pittsburgh: University of Pittsburgh Press, 1966), and James L. Payne, *Patterns of Conflict in Colombia* (New Haven: Yale University Press, 1968).

18. Jesús María Henao and Gerardo Arrubla, Historia de Colombia, 8th edn. (Bogotá: Talleres Editoriales de la Librería Voluntad, 1967), 695.

19. Germán Colmenares, *Partidos políticos y classes sociales* (Bogotá: Ediciones Universidad de los Andes, 1968), 100, my translation.

20. Orlando Fals Borda, *Subversión y cambio social* (Bogotá: Ediciones Tercer Mundo, 1968), 101–102, my translation.

21. Leal, "Social Classes," 88–89.

22. Ibid., 100.

23. Henao and Arrubla, *Historia de Colombia*, my translation.

24. Ibid., 815.

25. Santa, *Sociología política*, 37, my translation.

26. These coalitions are discussed in Harvey F. Kline, "The National Front: Historical Perspective and Overview," in R. Albert Berry, Ronald G. Hellman, and Mauricio Solaún (eds.), *Politics of Compromise: Coalition Government in Colombia* (New Brunswick, N.J.: Transaction Books, 1980), 59–83.

27. Henao and Arrubla, *Historia de Colombia*, 689.

28. Jaime Jaramillo Uribe, "Etapas y sentido de la historia de Colombia," in Mario Arrubla et al., *Colombia hoy* (Bogotá: Siglo Veiniuno Editores, 1980), 46.

29. Leal, "Social Classes," 112.

30. Helen Delpar, "Aspects of Liberal Factionalism in Colombia, 1875–1885," *Hispanic American Historical Review* 51 (May 1971):273.

31. See Chapter 6 for a more detailed discussion. These events are summarized, among other places, in Federico Gil, *Latin American–United States Relations* (New York: Harcourt Brace Jovanovich, 1971), 126–133.

32. Leal, "Social Classes," 228; J. Fred Rippy, *The Capitalists and Colombia* (New York: Vanguard Press, 1931), 103–122.

33. Justo Ramón S.C., *Historia de Colombia: Significado de su obra colonial, independencia y república* (Bogotá: n.p., 1962), 357.

34. Robert H. Dix, *Colombia: The Political Dimensions of Change* (New Haven: Yale University Press, 1967), 130.

35. Alfonso López Michelsen, "Del origen de la violencia en Colombia," *El Tiempo* (Bogotá), July 14, 1991, my translation.

3

PARTISAN CONFLICT, 1930–1974

THE PERIOD IN COLOMBIAN politics from 1930–1974 was one of constant partisan contention: sectarian democracy, civil war (including the most violent and longest in Colombian history), military dictatorship, "consociational democracy," and marxist guerrilla warfare. Throughout these years the key actors were the elite sectors of the two political parties. Colombian society was undergoing dramatic changes, and political leaders disagreed on how to deal with them.

Population growth, especially after World War II, brought increased conflict over land and migration to the major cities. In those cities, migrants faced a different world, with new opportunities and less influence of the church and the landowners. Parts of the Liberal party reacted to these changes by calling for a new role for the state; parts of the Conservative party summoned Colombians to return with them to the past. Majorities of both parties took a middle ground, hoping to preserve traditional influence while making marginal changes in the luck of the poor.

Conflict and Violence, 1930–1958

The period began with a change of party hegemony. Things were not going well for the Conservatives, not only because of the Great Depression but also because of their use of the army in 1928 to repress a strike of banana workers in Santa Marta. In 1930 they offered two presidential candidates, and the Liberals (together with the Moderate Conservatives) offered Enrique Olaya Herrera, then ambassador to Washington. As had happened in the past (and would happen again), the party of the presidency changed when the dominant party could not agree on a single candidate.

Under the stipulations of the Constitution of 1886, a change of party in the presidency inevitably led to a change in law-enforcement policy, because the president appointed all the governors (who in turn named all the mayors of the municipalities in their departments) and all cabinet and subcabinet officials. In the highly partisan Colombian political world, Conservative police officers (appointed by Conservative mayors or governors) were more likely to apply the strict letter of the law to Liberals and vice versa. The election of Olaya led to violence between the two parties and to clashes between police and peasants attempting to improve their land-tenure situations that proved a harbinger of things to come.

Liberal Hegemony, 1930–1946

Factionalism had always been common, but after 1930 its ideologies and social bases changed. In general, by 1930 the disputes of the previous century about federalism versus centralism had been settled or at least set aside. The new element was the dispute over the role of the state in the economy. Some members of the Liberal party had become advocates of government intervention in the economy and of controlled social change. This change of party program had first been suggested by Rafael Uribe Uribe at the beginning of the century but was not adopted by a party convention until 1922.[1] The Liberals were not united in this ideology, however, and the Conservatives opposed it. The Historical Conservatives often invoked a corporate-organic state paradigm and called for a return to the glories of Ferdinand and Isabella of sixteenth-century Spain. Moderate (as opposed to Radical) Liberals and the Moderate Conservatives favored the status quo and advocated neither a larger role for the state in the economy nor an organic state. The two moderate groups were prone to enter into coalitions, often against the extremists of their own parties. These divisions continue to the present.

Yet ideology was not the only factor in factionalism. For one thing, factional conflicts involved leaders with forceful personalities that inspired personal animosities. Since many of these leaders headed their factions for long periods of time, these conflicts tended to be long-lasting. For example, Laureano Gómez was the leader of the Historical Conservatives from 1930 to the 1960s. The man who followed him, his son Alvaro, remained a leader into the 1990s. Mariano Ospina led the Moderate Conservatives from 1930 to 1958. Alberto Lleras Camargo first led the Moderate Liberals in 1945 and was still part of the leadership in the 1970s. The Radical Liberals were first led by Alfonso López Pumarejo and Jorge Eliécer Gaitán, and their iron man, Carlos Lleras Restrepo, led the faction from the 1950s to the 1980s, when he was succeeded by a protégé, Luis Carlos Galán.

Another factor in factionalism was patronage. Because all government jobs were part of a spoils system (it was reported that they changed with the party—or faction—in power all the way down to the maids and doorkeepers in the governmental offices), conflicts occurred over whose followers would get them. Colombian politics continued to center around *roscas,* the personal cliques that included not only highly educated people who might fill ministerial posts but also people of lower social groups who could occupy all kinds of other positions.

Lastly, there was differentiation by class. The Radical Liberals represented the new financial-capital groups, the Historical Conservatives the traditional *latifundistas,* and the moderate factions of each party such more ambiguous sectors as the export-oriented landowners and the trade associations.[2] The role of the "popular" classes remained secondary except for the emergence of organized labor. Although Olaya's was a status-quo government in coalition with the Moderate Conservatives, it did recognize the right of workers to form unions for the first time with Law 83 of 1931. More important, it actively supported union organization and intervened in favor of workers in certain strikes. This brought it into conflict with some elements of the Conservative party, especially Gómez's factions.[3]

Olaya was followed in 1934 by Alfonso López Pumarejo, whose presidency is commonly called the "Revolution on the March." During his tenure the state was given a constitutionally guaranteed role in economic development and diversification of exports. Legal measures were enacted to protect domestic industry, credit institutions were strengthened, and a graduated income tax and taxes on excess profits and patrimony were introduced. Labor became a "social obligation" with the special protection of the state. The right to strike was guaranteed, and a series of laws gave unions firmer guarantees in collective bargaining. This mobilization of labor had two main purposes: to provide the president's party with a broader support base and to help ensure his control of the Liberal party.[4] Although he failed to do either, labor became a new actor in the political arena, and party divisions over this new protagonist worsened.

Property was expected to perform a social function, and property not being used effectively could be expropriated. Law 200 of 1936 stated that a presumption of ownership existed in favor of those who occupied the land and made economic use of it. Squatters could not be evicted unless the owner could prove title prior to 1821. All privately owned lands that remained uncultivated for the next ten consecutive years were to revert to the public domain.

National expenditures for education increased fourfold during the López presidency. Primary education, previously a municipal and departmental responsibility, was brought under national control. Primary education became obligatory, the national university was strengthened, and normal schools were established.[5]

The López Revolution on the March aggravated the factional divisions within the president's party; by the time of the 1937 congressional elections, a real and lasting split had occurred among Liberals. So serious was the opposition from his own party in the following congressional sessions that in May 1937 López threatened to resign.[6] The leadership of the Moderate Liberals was assumed by Eduardo

Santos, owner and editor of the newspaper *El Tiempo.* His followers fought the López programs in Congress, often joining the Conservatives to do so,[7] and he was elected president in 1938. The Santos administration sought neither to pursue the López reforms nor, more important, to rescind them. In many cases, such action was probably unnecessary, as policy implementation had never been effective. Similarly, the administration was characterized more by benign neglect than by active opposition to organized labor.[8]

Although López returned to the presidency in 1942, his second term has been called "the reform of the reformer." The prevailing economic conditions were not auspicious for reform; the moderate factions of the two parties had a majority in the Congress that could effectively block it, and opposition groups were able to capitalize on a series of "improprieties" of the López family (although not of the president himself) to keep the president constantly on the defensive.[9] In 1944 López was seized by the garrison in Pasto, and even though the rest of the military supported him he resigned in 1945, a full year before the end of his term. His replacement, Alberto Lleras Camargo, repressed such strikes as occurred during the interregnum. In an attempt to restore Liberal party unity, Lleras quickly broke the most important militant and Communist-dominated unions. However, his efforts at unity were frustrated by opposition both from the Santos moderate wing and from an increasingly radical one.[10]

The Liberal party split had progressed so far by 1946 that there were two party candidates in the election of that year: Gabriel Turbay, a moderate who received the endorsement of the party convention, and the Radical Jorge Eliécer Gaitán. Gaitán was a mestizo of lower-middle-sector background. He had first come to national attention by condemning the Conservative government for using the army in the UFCO strikes of 1928. He had a personal magnetism that some call charisma: One political leader has said that Gaitán had an uncanny ability to cause people to believe his every word. Gaitán was a populist who made the distinction between the *país político* (the political elite) and the *país nacional* (the real country, with its humble people).[11] He addressed that message to a country in which three-quarters of the population were peasants, more than half were illiterate, and 3 percent of the landowners owned half of the land. In response to the Lleras government's repression of strikes, Gaitán introduced two clearly reformist themes: economic redistribution and political participation.[12]

Until six weeks before the presidential election of 1946 there was no Conservative candidate. The last-minute candidacy of Mariano Ospina Pérez led to his election, although he did not receive a majority of the popular vote.

The Conservatives in Power and La Violencia

The Ospina government was a coalition with the Liberals. Ospina neither repressed the Liberal-backed unions nor recognized the Conservative one. His successor, Laureano Gómez, a Historical Conservative, was a reactionary and in the 1930s had been an unabashed supporter of Spain's Francisco Franco: "Spain, marching forward as the sole defender of Christian civilization, leads the Western nations in the reconstruction of empire of *Hispanidad,* and we inscribe our names in the roster of its phalanxes with unutterable satisfaction."[13] Although at one point he said, "I don't know how to do anything but foul things up,"[14] he sometimes blamed the Jews for the country's problems and expressed his disdain for majority rule through elections. It seemed clear to him that voting for Liberals would place Colombia behind the Iron Curtain.[15] Nevertheless, as president-elect, this "angry man of God" stated,

> I bless God a thousand and a thousand times for having filled my heart with this burning love for my country and for having made my mind grasp a sublime doctrine. . . . I praise God because he has permitted me to walk through the fires of hatred without allowing my heart to become contaminated by it, and has kept it happy, free from the dark shadows of vengeance, pure, without the dregs of bitterness.[16]

Gómez was elected president in 1949 (the presidential election having been called earlier than normal), but his term was short; for reasons of health he had to turn power over to the *designado* (a substitute elected for a two-year term by the Congress). Neither he nor Ospina had the opportunity to effect changes, as their attentions were monopolized by a growing civil war.

With the return of the Conservatives to power, violence had broken out almost immediately, especially in the departments of Santander, Norte de Santander, and Boyacá. In part this violence was caused by the change of party of law-enforcement officers. Conservative peasants could now seize the land of Liberals with impunity. Indeed, it is reported that in some cases they seized the very same lands in 1946–1947 that Liberal peasants had taken from them in 1930–1931. In addition, Conservative leaders at the local level tried to prevent Liberals from voting in the congressional elections of 1947.[17] Thus the pattern established in the nineteenth century persisted: Violence was viewed as justified by political and religious goals. Yet the partisan conflict generally known as La Violencia[18] was different in that it combined social, economic, and political aspects. Different areas were affected in different ways by social conflicts between campesinos (called *chusma,* "riffraff," by the government) and large landowners over land, struggles over crops, and party conflicts.[19]

The incipient violence was aggravated by the assassination of Jorge Gaitán in the streets of Bogotá on April 9, 1948, which brought several days of turmoil in the major cities (including the *bogotazo,* the extremely destructive and deadly violence in Bogotá, during which mobs burned churches). It was, however, primarily a rural phenomenon, and it continued, albeit with greater or lesser intensity, for nearly twenty years.[20] The church took the side of the Conservative government. According to the Colombian historian Gonzalo Sánchez,

> After April 9 the Church breathed holy ire. In a country that called itself the most Catholic in the world, the Church's authority had been wounded, its properties ravaged, its personnel abused. . . . In consequence, although with some notable excep-

tions, the Church put all of its institutional weight on the side of governmental power. It simultaneously anathematized the opposition and offered the Kingdom of God to the government's terrorist bands.[21]

Parish priests refused the sacraments to Liberals, and at least one bishop threatened to excommunicate people who voted Liberal.[22] With the exception of southernmost Nariño, almost all of the Andean part of the country was affected, as were the Orinoco Plains. The Caribbean coast was little involved; politics was taken less seriously in that part of the country, and the Liberal party had an overwhelming majority. In the beginning, La Violencia followed party lines; Conservatives attacked Liberals and vice versa.

Nor surprisingly, the law-enforcement agencies of the Conservative governments—the national police and the army—took the Conservative side in the conflict; police and army detachments descended like cyclones to terrorize defenseless towns.[23] Increasingly, however, other conflicts became possible because of the absence of effective law enforcement. The Colombian state had never been strong, the country never having accepted that the state should give form to the social order.[24] (This "partial breakdown of the state," as Oquist describes it,[25] was to be repeated in the 1980s.) All kinds of latent agrarian conflicts emerged—over good crop lands, water rights, and long-standing grievances. Almost all of La Violencia was between campesinos. In contrast to the civil wars of the nineteenth century, the violence this time was incited by political leaders and landowners who did not themselves participate in it.[26] Campesino violence against landowners was infrequent. From a marxist point of view, La Violencia was based on false consciousness; from a Colombian point of view it was a logical extension of patterns learned during nearly a century of partisan conflict.

One exception to this was in the Orinoco Plains, where a Law Organizing the Revolution on the Eastern Plains of Colombia was approved by a guerrilla assembly on June 18, 1953. The law's 224 articles were concerned with organization of the territory liberated by the Liberal guerrillas. It clearly envisioned the liberation of the entire country and the installation of a popular government: "The Revolution is a popular movement of liberation; it is the creation of all who participate in it." The law established a hierarchy of governing bodies: a congress ("the supreme authority of the Revolution"), a general staff, a commander in chief, zone commanders, and district councils. The councils were to be the primary organs of government, handling the organization and planning of production, the control of distribution, and the calling of monthly open meetings to discuss community problems. The law also established general guidelines for the war economy, in which private property was to be respected but a socialist tendency was dominant.[27]

Toward the end of La Violencia a new generation of young Colombians who had been socialized to think that violence was a normal way of life, finding themselves deprived of any legal way of earning a living, increasingly took to banditry. And in the 1960s some of the violence had revolutionary, class-oriented goals.

The Liberal hegemony and especially the López reforms had strengthened the state apparatus, and in the context of this enlarged state and sectarianism (the exclusion of the other party from the bureaucratic spoils), winning the presidency became a zero-sum game. The Conservatives sought to convert their party into a majority one, the Liberals to maintain their majority, and in the end at least 200,000 Colombians, mostly campesinos, died.

The Rojas Dictatorship

It was this context of systemic breakdown that produced Colombia's only twentieth-century military dictatorship. On June 13, 1953, when Laureano Gómez retook the active presidency from his *designado* and attempted to remove the military commander, Lieutenant General Gustavo Rojas Pinilla, the latter staged a coup that ended the Gómez presidency and, for that matter, "democratic" government until 1958. (Increasingly, the Conservative government had not been democratic in any meaningful way; today many Colombians refer to the "Gómez dictatorship.") The Rojas coup was welcomed by the elite of both political parties (with the obvious exception of the deposed Historical Conservatives). This bipartisan support was to last for several years, although Rojas, who considered himself a Conservative, received his most active support from the Moderates of that party.

The Rojas government took immediate steps to bring an end to La Violencia. In return for amnesty and government aid, many of the guerrilla bands ceased fighting. An effort was made to depoliticize the national police by transferring it to the armed forces (it had been part of the Ministry of the Interior). Press censorship was relaxed; political prisoners were released. In addition, the government started an extensive series of public-works projects and improved the system of credits for small farmers.[28] Clothing and food were given to the poor through a National Secretariat of Social Assistance (Secretariado Nacional de Asistencia Social, SENDAS). Rojas's motives have been debated: Some see him as concerned with breaking the power of the traditional party elites, others as an opportunist. What seems clear is that the lull in La Violencia was only temporary and the dictatorship produced no structural realignment of Colombian society.

The partisan elite (with the exception of the Moderate Conservatives) became increasingly restive, especially after Rojas called a national convention to draft a new constitution and began talking about a "third force" (a vague coalition of all groups of society patterned as was his dictatorship after the Perón experience in Argentina) and after it became increasingly clear that Rojas was not going to hold the 1958 presidential election. It is intriguing that, a decade and a half later, Colombian congressmen better remembered the "lack of the normal rules of the political game" during the Rojas years than La Violencia.[29]

There were abuses of government that were blamed on Rojas, whether or not he was personally at fault. These included the "Bullring Massacre" of February 5, 1956, when government-hired thugs beat and killed fans who failed to cheer for Rojas at a Sunday afternoon bullfight. Press censorship returned. By early 1957, most organized groups were opposed to Rojas. The parties were planning a coalition government; the church had lost interest in the Rojas experiment. The leaders of most of the trade associations had supported the labor unions in general strikes.[30] On May 10, 1957, the top military leaders asked Rojas to leave the country. After his departure, these leaders formed a caretaker military junta to govern until August 7, 1958.

The National Front, 1958–1974

Origin and Stipulations

The next sixteen years were ones of power sharing between the two traditional parties. This agreement, called the Frente Nacional (National Front), similar to agreements in ethnically divided nations such as Belgium, Cyprus, and Lebanon, has been called "consociational democracy."[31]

While some argue that the National Front government was inspired by the ideas of former president Alfonso López Pumarejo, the specific path of coalition government evolved through two meetings in Spain of former presidents Laureano Gómez and Alberto Lleras, two agreements signed in Bogotá, and a last-minute change caused by Conservative factionalism. In the end, almost all members of the party elites agreed on the coalition.

The first meeting was in Benidorm, Spain, in 1956, while Rojas was still in power. The two leaders there agreed on five points: (1) that common action by the Liberal and Conservative parties was needed to ensure the quickest possible return to civilian, democratic government; (2) that the two parties must share the blame for the violence and the breakdown of political order; (3) that the military should be returned to the role of protecting the country from external aggression and internal disturbances; (4) the coalition government or a series of coalition governments would have to be established; and (5) that Colombia was "infertile land for dictatorship."[32] Although the Benidorm rhetoric suggested that the two parties were united behind this agreement, the Moderate Conservatives, headed by Mariano Ospina Pérez, were still cooperating with the Rojas government.

This factional dispute between Ospina and Gómez, surely not a new one, continued to prevent agreement. In 1957 the *ospinistas*, for the first time excluded from the military government, signed another agreement with the Liberals. Called the March Pact, it differed in language but not in substance from the Pact of Benidorm. However, in the end the followers of Laureano Gómez refused to sign it.

The third pact in the series (and the second signed in Spain) was the 1957 one agreed to in Sitges, once again by Gómez and Lleras. The original goal of ridding Colombia of the military dictatorship had disappeared with the fall of Rojas earlier in the year. The Sitges Pact (once again, between Liberals and Gómez Conservatives) stipulated that the first president under the coalition government would be a Conservative. Internal conflicts within the Conservative party led to a fourth and last pact, that of San Carlos, signed by the leadership of all party factions. The main stipulation added by San Carlos was that the Conservative candidate be chosen by the Congress, which would be elected before the president.

The results of these agreements were then submitted to the people of Colombia, who overwhelmingly approved them as constitutional amendments in a December 1957 plebiscite. Soon afterward, congressional elections were held. The Gómez Conservatives emerged from that election as the largest Conservative faction in Congress, effectively vetoing the candidacy of Guillermo León Valencia (until then the strongest Conservative presidential candidate). After negotiation, the top faction leaders agreed that the first president would be a Liberal and that the coalition would be extended from twelve to sixteen years. This final agreement and the other stipulations of the plebiscite were ratified by the Congress as a constitutional amendment in 1958.

The National Front had the following characteristics:

1. The presidency would alternate every four years between the two traditional parties.
2. All legislative bodies (Congress, departmental assemblies, and municipal councils) would be divided equally between the Liberals and Conservatives regardless of the electoral results within a district (parity). Within each of the two traditional parties, seats would be assigned by a list form of proportional representation.
3. This same rule of parity would apply to all administrative appointments not under civil service, such as the presidential cabinet, gubernatorial cabinets, governors, mayors, and others.
4. No parties other than the Liberal and the Conservative could take part in elections.
5. The civil-service component of the bureaucracy would expand to cover all but the highest appointments. Partisan criteria would not enter into the selection of civil servants.
6. All legislation had to be passed by a two-thirds majority in the Congress.
7. A minimum of 10 percent of the national budget had to go to education.
8. Women were to have equal political rights. (General Rojas's government had declared female suffrage in 1954, but of course there had been no elections in which to vote.)

In essence, the National Front was a constitutional mechanism designed to divide *all* national power equally between the two parties.

Party Politics Under the National Front

The Colombian party leaders had engaged in political engineering to end military government and to eliminate the competition between the parties that had produced La Violencia. Although the Front was successful in both of these goals, it had other effects that were apparently unanticipated or considered unimportant at the time.

Factional Competition. To the surprise of many, this undemocratic experiment lasted the full sixteen years. Two Liberal presidents (Alberto Lleras Camargo, 1958–1962; Carlos Lleras Restrepo, 1966–1970), and two Conservatives (Guillermo León Valencia, 1962–1966; Misael Pastrana Borrero, 1970–1974) were elected. The stipulations of parity were honored, and the Congress, the departmental assemblies, and the more than eight hundred municipal councils were divided equally between Liberals and Conservatives (although it was reported that some small rural *municipios* had difficulty in finding a full complement of one party or the other for their councils). The governors were divided equally; the presidential cabinet was also equally divided, with the military minister of defense making such a division of thirteen possible. Various laws were passed to develop a more extensive civil service. Non-civil-service bureaucrats (the majority) were also divided equally.

Political competition during the National Front years was factional competition. The institutional framework it established allowed factions to flourish as never before. As the president in any election had to be from a certain party and the legislative bodies were divided equally between the parties regardless of the popular vote, there were no *party* disincentives for factional divisions. As mentioned above, there could be no new political parties, but "party" was defined in such a way that any group could offer candidates as long as it did not call itself a party. Hence, in addition to the continued divisions between Gómez followers (earlier called Historical Conservatives and Doctrinaire Conservatives and later called Independent Conservatives) and Ospina followers (during these years called Unionist Conservatives) and the "Official" Liberals, two new groups appeared and were allowed to offer candidates. The first was the Revolutionary Liberal Movement (Movimiento Revolucionario Liberal, MRL), founded in 1960. It was led by Alfonso López Michelsen (son of the former president). The MRL opposed the National Front and advocated more rapid socioeconomic reforms. It disbanded in 1967, when López rejoined the "Official" Liberals. A longer-lasting group was the National Popular Alliance (Alianza Nacional Popular, ANAPO), founded in 1961 by former dictator Rojas Pinilla. ANAPO offered both Conservative and Liberal candidates for the Congress (the Conservatives being notably more successful), a Liberal candidate for president in 1966, and a Conservative one (Rojas himself) in 1970. The apogee of ANAPO was in the 1970 election, in which its Liberal lists governed 14 percent of the congressional votes and its Conservative lists 20 percent; Rojas lost the presidential election by only 3 percent of the vote. (Indeed, there are some who think that the election was stolen from Rojas by fraud in vote counting.) In 1971 ANAPO declared itself a political party, and thereafter its fortunes rapidly declined. Rojas died in 1975, and for all intents and purposes his "party" also died.

In congressional elections extreme factionalism meant a great diversity of choice for the electors. One could vote for a list identified with one of the major factions of the Conservatives or for one representing the Liberal factions (and ANAPO had both). Furthermore, these factions might offer more than one list, either approved by the departmental leadership (an "official" list) or not (a "dissident" list). In the 1968 lower-house election, for example, there were 111 Liberal and 108 Conservative lists of candidates in the twenty-three electoral districts (corresponding to departments). The multiplicity of lists was more pronounced in some departments than in others; the most extreme case was in Nariño, in which there were 10 Liberal and 8 Conservative lists.[33]

In presidential elections, several candidates usually ran. Sometimes these candidates were "illegal" in that they were not from the party that constitutionally was to win the presidency that year (for example, Alfonso López Michelsen ran in 1962 as a Liberal MRL candidate). At other times there was little suspense even though there was more than one legal candidate (for example, in 1966 Carlos Lleras Restrepo had only token ANAPO opposition). By far the most competitive election was in 1970, when there were four major Conservative candidates. The National Front candidate was Misael Pastrana, who, in the absence of Conservative agreement, was chosen by the Liberal party convention. Pastrana, himself a Unionist, was opposed by Rojas from ANAPO and by two Independent Conservatives: Evaristo Sourdís and Belisario Betancur. In this four-candidate election, Pastrana won with 36 percent of the vote.

Despite all of this electoral choice (or perhaps because of it) in congressional elections, Colombian voters abstained in large numbers. The percentage of eligible voters exercising their franchise in congressional elections fell from a high of 60 percent in 1958 to a low of 31 in 1968. In presidential elections the percentages ranged from 50 in 1958 to 34 in 1966.[34]

Perhaps more intriguing than this decline in voting was the agonizing over it of the political elite. The party leaders had, after all, engineered a system designed to end one form of political behavior—violence—and therefore it is not terribly surprising that it ended another kind—voting. In a situation in which the Congress and other elected assemblies would be divided equally between the two parties and the presidency would alternate, the only two possible reasons to vote were that one had a sense of civic responsibility and that one favored one faction of a political party more than another. Public-opinion data indicate that the people of Colombia in general have never developed an identification with a faction; most simply report being either Conservatives or Liberals. The vote therefore had little marginal benefit except when there was a protest candidate. Groups on the left concluded, however, that the decline in voting was a sign of alienation and that Colombians would, when they could, vote for more radical alternatives. This did not happen until 1990. Further, it can be argued that abstention rates during the National Front were no higher than they had been historically in Colombia, especially when one considers that women, as new voters, were voting less than men.[35]

Immobilism. The founders of the National Front realized that they were engineering a system in which public policymaking would be severely constrained. As Alberto Lleras told the people of Colombia in his New Year's address of 1959, the Front would "do everything that the two parties had said should be done, but that each had not allowed the other to do, and not do for sixteen years what one of the parties might want to do against the will of the other."[36] It was Alberto Lleras who was most successful in policymaking, largely because his party was united and allied with the larger of the Conservative factions (the Gómez group for the first two years and the Ospina one for the next two, as electoral fortunes changed). With the growth of factionalism after his presidency, policymaking was more and more hampered, especially since a two-thirds vote was needed in the Congress.

This immobilism was increased by other characteristics of the National Front governments. The president was a lame duck almost from the beginning of his term. While this is a characteristic in any political system in which immediate reelection is prohibited, it was particularly acute where the president would necessarily be followed by a member of the *other* party. It seems reasonable to conclude that at least during the last two years of his term much more attention was paid to the president's possible successor than to his programs.

The president's cabinet was split into the various factions, including, during the Valencia presidency, both major Conservative groups. The non-civil-service bureaucracy was also split between factions; membership in a *rosca* of one of the factions was more important than technical expertise. A study in 1967 showed that, of the 100,000 government employees, only 3,000 were part of the civil service.[37] The others were evenly divided between the two parties and in some cases between the various factions of the parties.

Economic interest groups, in this chaotic situation, were very effective in blocking any legislation that disfavored them because of their contacts with members of Congress and bureaucrats. To be passed a legislative proposal needed the support of the president and his cabinet and two-thirds of the Congress. To be *implemented* it needed technically proficient bureaucrats unhampered by political interests and family and friendship ties. Under the circumstances, it is not surprising that the National Front governments made few policy changes in the direction of redistribution. Yet the National Front did allow insulation of economic policymakers from partisan politics, and its most notable success was ending La Violencia.

Constitutional Reform. One response to this immobilism was the Constitutional Reform of 1968, which ended the two-thirds vote requirement for congressional approval of legislation and strengthened the rule-making authority of the president to the detriment of the Congress. In addition, the reform's Article 120 ended some of the National Front stipulations while extending others. This was popularly called the dismantling (*desmonte*) of the National Front.

Under its terms, cabinet ministries, the offices of governors and mayors, and other administrative positions that were not part of the civil service were to be divided equally between Liberals and Conservatives until August 7, 1978—four years after the termination of the National Front. After that date these offices were to be divided between the parties in such a way as to provide "adequate and equitable participation to the major party distinct from that of the president." However, if that nonpresidential party decided not to participate in the executive, the president would be free to name the officials in any way he chose. Elective legislative bodies were no longer to be divided equally. Departmental assemblies and municipal councils became completely competitive in 1970, the Congress in 1974. New political parties could participate in elections where the rule of parity did not exist beginning in 1970 and in all elections from 1974 on.

The reform might best be seen as a compromise. Some Colombian political leaders favored an extension of the National Front. Others even talked about a combination of Liberals and Conservatives in a Colombian version of the Mexican Partido Revolucionario Institucional (PRI). Still others favored a return to complete competition. The debate over Article 120 continued until it was eliminated by the Constitution of 1991.

Conclusion

By 1958 it had become clear that Colombia was not ready for complete democracy; indeed, Alberto Lleras had stated as early as 1946 that the only way to end the violence associated with democratic competition was through coalition government. The National Front did bring to an end the traditional partisan violence, and many feared that the end of it would lead to new outbreaks of Liberal-Conservative violence. It is understandable, then, that the Constitutional Reform of 1968 was to some extent a compromise.

In large part, La Violencia was the logical result of nearly a century of sectarian democracy. In the same way, the National Front was a logical solution to La Violencia. But social and economic conflicts also contributed to the violence, and the immobilism of the National Front prevented the government from resolving those conflicts. By 1974 sixteen years of coalition government had produced (1) a lack of political space for individuals attracted to neither the Liberals nor the Conservatives, (2) a failure to resolve a number of key economic problems of underdevelopment, (3) continued violence in the countryside, although no longer in the name of traditional party, (4) a dearth of the economic resources that might allow the poor to earn a decent wage, (5) a relatively small group of political and economic leaders living very well in the cities, (6) a government even less able to enforce its laws than before, and (7) a weak and politically divided labor movement, while the great majority of the urban and rural poor were not organized at all. All of these problems were to be exacerbated as Colombia arrived at the edge of chaos.

Notes

1. Fals Borda, *Subversión y cambio social,* 130.

2. Bruce Michael Bagley, "Political Power, Public Policy, and the State in Colombia: Case Studies of the Urban and Agrarian Reforms during the National Front, 1958–1974" (Ph.D. diss., University of California, Los Angeles, 1979), 48–60.

3. Ruth Bergins Collier and David Collier, *Shaping the Political Arena: Critical Junctures, the Labor Movement, and Regime Dynamics in Latin America* (Princeton: Princeton University Press, 1991), 290.

4. Ibid., 292.

5. Dix, *Colombia,* 87–89.

6. Ibid., 91.

7. Fluharty, *Dance of the Millions,* 57.

8. Collier and Collier, *Shaping the Political Arena,* 293.

9. John D. Martz, *Colombia: A Contemporary Political Survey* (Chapel Hill: University of North Carolina Press, 1962), 38–41.

10. Collier and Collier, *Shaping the Political Arena,* 295.

11. The political leader quoted came from a confidential interview with a Liberal senator, May 28, 1981. An excellent biography of Gaitán in English is Richard E. Sharpless, *Gaitán of Colombia: A Political Biography* (Pittsburgh: University of Pittsburgh Press, 1978).

12. Gonzalo Sánchez, "The Violence: An Interpretative Synthesis," in Charles Berquist, Ricardo Peñaranda, and Gonzalo Sánchez (eds.), *Violence in Colombia: The Contemporary Crisis in Historical Perspective* (Wilmington, Del.: Scholarly Resources, Inc., 1992), 77.

13. Dix, *Colombia,* 109, citing Germán Arciniegas, *The State of Latin America,* trans. Harriet de Onis (New York: Alfred A. Knopf, 1952), 163.

14. Alexander W. Wilde, "Conversations Among Gentlemen: Oligarchical Democracy in Colombia," in Juan J. Linz and Alfred Stepan (eds.), *The Breakdown of Democratic Regimes: Latin America* (Baltimore: Johns Hopkins University Press, 1978), 56, citing Augusto Ramírez Moreno, *La crisis del Partido Conservador* (Bogotá n.p., 1937), 25.

15. Sánchez, "The Violence," 86.

16. Martz, *Colombia,* 96–97, quoting Arciniegas, *The State of Latin America,* 176.

17. The most complete Colombian study, including documents that show this elite instigation, is Germán Guzmán Campos, Orlando Fals Borda, and Eduardo Umaña Luna, *La violencia en Colombia,* 2 vols. (Bogotá: Ediciones Tercer Mundo, 1962, 1964).

18. While the term *la violencia* means simply "the violence," for most Colombians it refers specifically to this period. There is, however, considerable disagreement about when it began (some say 1946, others 1948) and, to a lesser degree, when it ended.

19. Alvaro Camacho Guizado, "El ayer y el hoy de la violencia en Colombia: Continuidades y discontinuidades," *Análisis Político*, no. 12 (January–April 1991): 24–25.

20. In terms of the number of deaths per year, Paul Oquist (*Violence, Conflict, and Politics in Colombia* [New York: Academic Press, 1980], 9) argues, 1966 was the last year of the violence begun in 1946.

21. Sánchez, "The Violence," 87.

22. Guzmán, Fals Borda, and Umaña, *La violencia*, vol. 1, 270–274.

23. Ibid., 89.

24. Daniel Pecaut, "Guerrillas and Violence," in Berquist, Peñaranda, and Sánchez, *Violence in Colombia*, 222.

25. Oquist, *Violence, Conflict, and Politics*, Chapter 5.

26. Sánchez, "The Violence," 91.

27. Ibid., 95–96.

28. Dix, *Colombia*, 117–118.

29. Harvey F. Kline, "Selección de candidatos," in Gary Hoskin, Francisco Leal, Harvey Kline, Dora Rothlisberger, and Armando Borrero, *Estudio del comportamiento legislativo en Colombia* (Bogotá: Editorial Universidad de los Andes, 1975), 173.

30. Jonathan Hartlyn, "Interest Groups and Political Conflict in Colombia: A Retrospective and Prospective View," paper presented at the U.S. State Department Conference on Colombia, Washington, D.C., November 9, 1981, 4.

31. The best study of this for the Colombian case is Jonathan Hartlyn, *The Politics of Coalition Rule in Colombia* (Cambridge: Cambridge University Press, 1988).

32. Miles Wendell Williams, "El Frente Nacional: Colombia's Experiment in Controlled Democracy" (Ph.D. diss., Vanderbilt University, 1972), 78, citing Guillermo Hernández Rodriguez, *La alternación ante el pueblo como constituyente primario* (Bogotá: n.p., 1962), 12–16.

33. Harvey F. Kline, "The Cohesion of Political Parties in the Colombian Congress: A Case Study of the 1968 Session" (Ph.D. diss., University of Texas, 1970), 68.

34. Rodrigo Losada, "Electoral Participation," in Berry, Hellman, and Solaún, *Politics of Compromise*, 90, 95.

35. Ibid., 90.

36. Alberto Lleras Camargo, *Sus mejores páginas* (Bogotá: n.p., n.d.), 266, my translation.

37. Hartlyn, "Interest Groups," 25. He adds that, by 1976, only 13,000 people were part of the civil service.

4

THE EDGE OF CHAOS, 1974–1994

The period since 1974 has seen a completely new political regime in Colombia. Except for that of Virgilio Barco, all the administrations—all but one of them Liberal—have involved power sharing because of the Article 120 requirement of adequate and equitable participation for the minority party. The Barco administration might be called a "party government–loyal opposition democracy," and that regime encountered political difficulties.

On August 7, 1974, Alfonso López Michelsen was inaugurated as the first freely elected president of Colombia since Laureano Gómez (if Gómez could be considered as such, given the violence that prevented full Liberal participation in 1949). In an election in which all the major candidates were sons or daughters of former presidents, López received 56 percent of the vote, defeating both Conservative Alvaro Gómez and ANAPO candidate María Eugenia Rojas de Moreno Díaz. While López governed under the constraints of Article 120, he did have a Liberal Congress behind him. He was followed in 1978 by another Liberal, Julio César Turbay Ayala, who had narrowly defeated the Conservative Belisario Betancur. Turbay also had a Liberal majority in Congress, and he chose to give governmental positions to both major factions of the Conservative party. Turbay's solution to social unrest was repression,[1] and his government was the most authoritarian in Colombia since the 1950s.

In 1982, Belisario Betancur won the presidency (with 47 percent of the vote) over two Liberal candidates, Alfonso López Michelsen and Luis Carlos Galán. This election showed a clear continuation of the historical pattern of a division of the majority party's allowing the minority party to win the presidency. Liberals recovered the presidency in 1986, when Virgilio Barco won with 58 percent of the vote over the Conservative Alvaro Gómez Hurtado. During the campaign Barco had called for a party government in the face of the requirements of Article 120. His offer of three cabinet posts to the Conservatives was rejected by their leadership as failing the constitutional test of adequate and equitable representation. The Conservatives instead embarked on what Misael Pastrana called "thoughtful opposition."

It soon became obvious that this government-and-loyal-opposition regime, never before experienced in Colombia, was not working well. On the one hand, the Liberal party was what one of its leaders called a "stewpot of scorpions,"[2] many of its members of Congress paying more attention to regional leaders than to national ones. On the other, the Conservatives were also divided, some even opposing "thoughtful opposition." On the Liberal side, President Barco never developed the personal ties with members of Congress that a real party leader needed. Perhaps most important, although both Barco and Pastrana agreed that some issues of the "dirty war" were of such importance that the two parties would have to work together, they never reached an agreement on which specific issues they were. His presidency proved to be one of the bloodiest in Colombian history. Guerrillas and paramilitaries—assisted at times by the government—confronted each other; other paramilitary groups, established by the drug dealers, fought the guerrillas and the government. So-called clean-up squads—private citizens, usually young male members of the upper class—conducted sweeps to rid the cities of "undesirables" such as gays, addicts, and the homeless. The government was too weak to control these groups, and even common criminals were free to kill, rob, and kidnap with near complete impunity. Just as in the partisan La Violencia, there had been a breakdown of the state.

The presidential election of 1990 saw the assassination of three candidates. Luis Carlos Galán, the leading Liberal, was assassinated by drug-related groups in August 1989. Bernardo Jaramillo, the candidate of the Unión Patriótica, was assassinated in March 1990 and Carlos Pizarro Leongómez, the candidate of the Alianza Democrática M-19, in April. In both cases drug dealers were blamed. César Gaviria, a Liberal follower of Galán, was elected president. Gaviria was the first presidential candidate to be chosen by the Liberals through a new "popular consulting" process whereby the congressional elections included the choice of a presidential candidate. Gaviria returned to the spirit of Article 120, inviting not only Conservatives to join his cabinet but also a member of the AD-M19. At the same time, he was instrumental in leading the country to the establishment of a constituent assembly to write a new constitution that among other things eliminated the requirement of joint government.

Gaviria was followed by the Liberal Ernesto Samper, who defeated the Conservative Andrés Pastrana in the first-ever two-round presidential election.

After leading Pastrana by only 0.3 percent in the first round, Samper won the second with 51 percent of the vote. While the administrations in Bogotá came and went, violence flourished in the countryside.[3]

Guerrillas

The years since the National Front have seen four major guerrilla organizations in Colombia: the Revolutionary Armed Forces of Colombia (Fuerzas Armadas de la Revoluciónarias Colombianas, FARC), the National Liberation Army (Ejército de Liberación Nacional, ELN), the People's Liberation Army (Ejército Popular de Liberación, EPL), and the Movimiento 19 de Abril (19th of April Movement, M-19). Estimates of the total number of insurgents have varied widely, from 4,000–5,000 in the early 1980s to 17,000 in 1984. Government officials in July 1992 reported 7,500, two-thirds in the FARC and one-third in the ELN.[4]

The ELN arose from a group of Colombian scholarship students who had arrived in Cuba at the height of the missile crisis and had asked for and received military training there and begun a series of discussions about a *foco* strategy (as called for by Che Guevara) for Colombia. Officially born on July 4, 1964, it was initially composed primarily of university students.[5] Since as early as 1949, the Communist party had been urging workers and peasants to defend themselves, and in that year Communists had joined Liberals in "resistance committees" opposing the Conservative government. The Alberto Lleras government initiated military actions in the Communist-influenced areas, but it was only in July 1964 that leaders from the east and south of Tolima met to constitute themselves as the "Southern Bloc." The FARC was founded two years later.[6] The pro-Chinese EPL had adopted the "prolonged people's war" strategy and was long close to extinction.[7] Although it came to an agreement with the government in 1990, a dissident faction refused to disarm and was still active in 1993.

The M-19, named for the date on which the election was "stolen" from Rojas Pinilla in 1970, had made its appearance in January 1974, when it stole a sword that had belonged to Bolívar from the collection of the Quinta de Bolívar. Its membership included dissidents expelled from the Communist party and the FARC and others from the socialist wing of ANAPO. They shared a belief in their struggle as a continuation of the crusade for freedom—a "second independence"—and a tendency to substitute audacious political-military feats for the patient work of building a political movement.[8] The M-19 began to be considered a serious urban guerrilla threat when it kidnapped and murdered the leader of the Confederation of Colombian Workers (Confederación de Trabajadores Colombianos, CTC) in early 1976. It receive international publicity when it tunneled into a Bogotá arsenal and stole arms in 1979, when it kidnapped all the guests (including the U.S. ambassador) attending a cocktail party at the Dominican embassy in Bogotá in 1980, and when it kidnapped and executed a missionary from the United States in 1981. Originally an urban guerrilla group, the M-19 also participated in rural activities in Chocó and the Nariño-Putumayo areas in 1981. Before 1990 the amount of support for the various guerrilla groups was open to speculation. While there was little doubt that the Colombian Communist party supported the FARC and various student groups promoted different guerrilla movements, there was no way to be certain of general support of the population.

During the López administration the government tried for the first time to open negotiations with the guerrillas. This effort was frustrated by the Colombian military's systematic blocking of any negotiations with the ELN, which the armed forces believed it could quickly annihilate.[9] Turbay also sought a nonviolent solution to the problem with amnesty offers (in March 1981 and February 1982) applying to all except those who had participated in "atrocious crimes" such as kidnapping, extortion, noncombat-related homicide, arson, the poisoning of water, and "acts of ferocity or barbarism."[10] These amnesties, however, had very limited success.

Within six weeks of his assuming office Belisario Betancur announced the formation of another Peace Commission, and Law 35 of 1982, signed by the president on November 20, granted amnesty to all those in armed conflict with the government before that date except those who had committed noncombat-related homicides or homicides that had included "cruelty" and in which the victim had been in a position of "inferior strength." Guerrillas already in jail for the pardoned crimes, whether indicted or convicted, were to be released. In the first three months some four hundred accepted the amnesty.[11] The Betancur initiative was based on the assumption that guerrilla violence could be understood as the product of the objective circumstances of poverty, injustice, and the lack of possibilities for political participation. It went on to include agreements with the FARC, the EPL, and the M-19 linked with the idea of a "national dialogue"—never very well defined but presumably having to do with government assistance to violence-affected areas. On April 1, 1984, the president announced an agreement with the FARC: a cease-fire for a period of one year, the creation of a "high-level commission" to verify the carrying out of the agreement, the granting of a series of juridical, political, and social guarantees to facilitate the return of the guerrillas to "democratic life," and a program of rehabilitation of the peasant areas affected by the violence. A similar truce was agreed to the following month with the M-19 and the EPL. Only the *fidelista* ELN had not signed a truce by the end of May 1984.[12]

By the end of 1985, however, two of the three truces had been broken, with leaders of the EPL and the M-19 accusing the government of causing the rupture and the government holding the guerrillas responsible. The M-19 announced its decision to return to combat on June 20, 1985; its leader, Alvaro Fayad, was quoted as saying, "The problem is that the oligarchy does not want to give up anything because they think that the solution for this country comes from submission and silencing not only of the guerrilla movement but also of the democratic sectors and of the new forces that want a different life."[13] On the morning of November 6, 1985, the M-19 seized the Palacio de Justicia in downtown Bogotá. By the time the army reestablished control the following day, a hundred people had died, including eleven of the twenty-four Supreme Court justices, and the Palacio had been gutted by fire. Although the FARC was still formally in truce at the end of Betancur's term, in fact hostilities had also resumed between that group and the government.

The Barco administration had greater success in the peace process. After the May 1988 kidnapping of Alvaro Gómez by M-19, Barco demonstrated more flexibility in the matter of negotiations, and in December 1989 the M-19 turned in its weapons and became a legal political party for the 1990 elections. The EPL also negotiated an agreement and demobilized. Gaviria's government continued conversations with the two remaining guerrilla groups in Caracas in 1991 and in Tlaxcala in 1992. Although an agreement was reached in 1994 with a small faction of the ELN (the Socialist Renovation Current [Corriente de Renovación Socialista]), talks with the larger groups were suspended during the last two Gaviria years. The FARC and ELN, working together through the Simón Bolívar Guerrilla Coordinator, continued their bombings of infrastructure (spilling more oil into the Orinoco River Basin than the Exxon Valdes did in Alaska) and kidnappings. This led in July 1991 to the first civilian demonstrations against the guerrilla activities. Since the breakdown of the negotiations in Tlaxcala in 1992 the guerrillas have turned to urban terrorism in an explicit attempt to hold the urban population hostage, as the Medellín drug group had earlier done. Investigative reporting by the weekly *Semana* in 1992 showed that the FARC and ELN had accumulated large amounts of money through kidnappings, the sale of protection to ranchers, and the cultivation and refining of coca and poppies. Instead of conversations with the guerrillas, the Gaviria government in its last two years stressed the training and equipping of counterinsurgency troops.

Drugs

Colombia's role in the international drug market developed very rapidly as a result of the major drug interdiction efforts launched by Mexico in 1975 at the urging of the U.S. government. As "the epicenter of marijuana production in the hemisphere," it was soon providing 70 percent of U.S. marijuana imports.[14] The cocaine trade, now using airplanes that employed traffic lanes already used by oil-rig pilots and others, increased dramatically; whereas in 1970 U.S. customs had seized only 100 kilograms of cocaine, in 1982 it seized 45 metric tonnes.[15] By 1979 Colombia was exporting some 37 metric tonnes (40.8 short tons) of cocaine and 15,000 tonnes (16,538 short tons) of marijuana. The Sierra Nevada region in

Caribbean coastal Colombia, including parts of the departments of Guajira, Cásar, and Magdalena, became the world's largest area of marijuana cultivation, by 1978 having 19,000 hectares (46,914 acres) in marijuana cultivation and employing some 18,500 people. One study concluded that the total earnings of Colombia's "other economy" in 1979 were US$3.2 billion. Of this total, US$2.15 billion (about 70 percent) came from marijuana, US$460 million (11 percent) from cocaine, and the remaining 11 percent from "traditional" contraband in coffee (US$150 million), sugar, cattle, and cement (US$440 million).[16] The small marijuana farmer received only about 7 percent of the total export value; most of the income from marijuana and cocaine was in the hands of a few.

Summarizing his conclusions in the early 1980s, one North American scholar stated that the illicit income earned by Colombians from all drug sales (1) contributed approximately 6 percent to the nation's 30 percent annual inflation rate and 15–18 percent to the growth of its money supply; (2) jeopardized Colombia's financial institutions and rendered precarious all forms of governmental economic planning; (3) diverted large sums of governmental funds, which were needed elsewhere, to the suppression of cultivation and trafficking; (4) contributed substantially to Colombia's becoming a food-importing country through the diversion of land and labor to drug production rather than that of staples; (5) reduced the funds available for legitimate lending and raised credit rates to the point that borrowers turned to extralegal sources (often traffickers of their colleagues) to secure financing; (6) contributed to increased tax evasion among a populace noted for not paying taxes; (7) penetrated and/or gained control of legitimate private corporations; (8) became the largest source of dollars in the underground economy and added millions to the nation's foreign-exchange surplus; and (9) grossly inflated the value of farm land, property, goods, services, and even art works in trafficking areas.[17] All of these trends were to become more important during the 1980s.

One response of the López administration to the drug trade was the opening of a *ventanilla siniestra* ("left-handed window") in the Banco de la República where anyone could exchange dollars for pesos with no questions asked. Other dollars entered the economy through the long-flourishing black market for dollars (but with an unusual twist: soon dollars were worth less on the black market than they were in official exchange). Many other dollars were simply not brought into the country but placed in banks and investments in other countries.

A new "trade association," called the *mafia* by Colombians and the "cartel" by foreigners, grew up around illicit drugs. At a national convention held secretly in December 1981, 223 drug-gang bosses are reported to have created a death squad called Death to Kidnappers (Muerte a Secuestradores, MAS) and pledged US$7.5 million to it. The squad's purpose was to put an end to the guerrilla practice of kidnapping people (including "honest hard-working drug-gang bosses") for ransom to finance their subversive activities.[18] This association was not a cartel in the strict economic sense, that is, a small group of producers who conspire to fix prices; there was more conflict than cooperation between the drug groups, especially between those of Medellín and Cali.

In the last half of the 1980s the drug dealers, using a carrot-and-stick approach, were able to paralyze the Colombian justice system. On the one hand, the judge who released the known drug leader Jorge Luis Ochoa from a Bogotá jail even though the U.S. Drug Enforcement Agency wanted his extradition was later charged with having taken a bribe. On the other, the judge contemplating the indictment of Pablo Escobar for the murder of the publisher of *El Espectador* received the following message signed "The Extraditables":

> We are friends of Pablo Escobar Gaviria and we are ready to do anything for him. . . . we know perfectly well that not even the slightest evidence exists against Mr. Escobar. We have also heard rumors that after the trial you will be given a foreign diplomatic position. But we want to remind you that, in addition to perpetrating a judicial infamy, you are making a big mistake. . . . we are capable of executing you at any place on this planet. . . . in the meantime you will see the fall, one by one, of all of the members of your family. We advise you to rethink it, for later you will have no time for regrets. . . . for calling Mr. Escobar to trial you will remain without forebears or descendants in your genealogical tree.[19]

Before Belisario Betancur became president, Colombian leaders had paid little or no attention to the drug trade, but during 1983 and early 1984 the Betancur government, led by Justice Minister Rodrigo Lara Bonilla, stepped up attacks on the drug centers and dealers. Lara suggested that drug money was being invested in legitimate enterprises, including professional soccer and bicycle racing, and accused several members of Congress of having received drug money for their campaigns.

The assassination of Lara on April 30, 1984, by thugs hired by the drug traffickers brought an immediate reaction: A state of siege was decreed for the entire country, raids were directed against the property of suspected drug dealers, including eighty in the city of Medellín alone, a program of aerial spraying of marijuana was begun, and an existing extradition treaty with the United States began to be enforced. By the end of 1984, 2,851,000 kilograms of marijuana and 23,931 kilograms of cocaine had been seized, 268 cocaine-processing laboratories destroyed, and 2,773 individuals arrested. None of the leading drug traffickers was seized, however. Seven of them (including Escobar and the Ochoa brothers) contacted former president Alfonso López Michelsen and National Procurator Carlos Jiménez Gómez from Panama and suggested a truce similar to the ones being signed with the guerrillas. They promised to desist from future drug trafficking and to bring US$2 billion to help pay the national debt if they were allowed to return to Colombia. The Betancur government declined the offer.

The Barco government alternated attacks on the drug dealers with attempts to negotiate with them. Periodically there were outbreaks of drug terrorism due, according to *Semana*, to the breakdowns of the talks (though the administration always insisted that there were no negotiations).[20] After the Galán assassination, the government declared war on the drug traffickers—destroying cocaine-producing laboratories, arresting and extraditing drug dealers, and seizing the property of suspected drug dealers. The drug dealers responded with bombings. Barco reported in his farewell address that his administration had won this war, but this was hyperbole. Between August 1989 and August 1990 over a thousand people died from the drug violence, including more than two hundred police in the city of Medellín alone. *Semana* did concede, however, that the drug dealers were in retreat.[21]

The dramatic new policy of the Gaviria administration was a negotiated solution whereby any drug trafficker could turn himself in, confess to at least one of his crimes (but not have to turn state's evidence on others), and receive reduced penalties for any crime for which he was convicted. Extradition had been ruled out by the new constitution. The Medellín drug leader Pablo Escobar turned himself in on June 19, 1991, and was incarcerated at a place that he had chosen, guarded by personnel whom he had chosen and apparently carrying out his drug business until July 22, 1992, when he escaped. It had been discovered that he was bringing members of his gang into the prison, to be judged and, if found disloyal, taken away and executed, and in response the government had decided to move him to a military prison. In the confusion of the transfer, involving the police, the army, and the air force, one of the most powerful men in the world drug trade walked out of the prison. Subsequent investigation revealed that while in prison Escobar had enjoyed the use of eleven telephone lines, a cellular telephone, and twenty carrier pigeons, each trained to return to a different part of the Medellín area.[22]

The Gaviria drug policy clearly did not end drug trafficking, but it did end the terrorism that had made 1990 the bloodiest year in Colombia's history. After Escobar's escape there were only a few notable cases of drug terrorism, and Escobar himself was killed in a gun battle with police and soldiers on December 2, 1993.

Death Squads

The Betancur years witnessed the rapid growth of paramilitary groups. Even the president admitted in October 1983 the paramilitaries were responsible for twice as many homicides as the guerrillas. The Colombian military was unhappy with the Betancur peace process, and documentation suggests that midrange officials assisted paramilitary groups with weapons, supplies, and training.[23] These groups varied from the ones set up by the drug dealers (including Death to Kidnappers) to "self-defense" groups organized with government assistance to combat guerrilla groups (most notable among these the one led by Henry de Jesús Pérez in Puerto Boyacá) and groups bent on ridding their cities of drug addicts, the homeless, and gays. Government sources suggested in the late 1980s that there were some 140 of these death squads. A partial list given by one Colombian sociologist included, in addition to the MAS, the Death Squad (El Escuadrón de la Muerte), The Group (El Grupo), Death to Rustlers (Muerte a Abiegos), Punishment to Swindling Intermediaries (Castigo a Firmantes e Intermediarios Estafadores), The Embryo (El Embrión), Alfa 83, Pro-Cleanup of the Magdalena Valley (Pro Limpieza del Valle de la Magdalena), The Soot-Faced (Los Tiznados), the Colombian Anticommunist Movement (Movimiento Anticomunista Colombiano), the Crickets (Los Grillos), the Machete Squadron (El Escuadrón Machete), Falange, Death to Land Invaders and Their Collaborators and Supporters (Muerte a Invasores, Colaboradores y Patrocinadores), and the Green Rangers (Los Comandos Verdes).[24] Knowledgeable members of the executive branch of government said in confidential interviews in July 1992 that neither army intelligence nor the security branch had good statistics on the number of death squads at that time. Several important ones in the Magdalena Medio and Córdoba turned in their arms in the 1991–1992 period under a plea-bargaining system similar to that with the drug traffickers. Many still existed, however, ranging in size from a few members to as many as 350.[25]

If there had been a partial breakdown of the state during La Violencia, there was now a second one. In addition to the drug dealers, guerrillas, and death squads, ordinary law breakers took advantage of the breakdown. The Colombian sociologist Alvaro Camacho calculated that 75 to 80 percent of the violence in Cali was "private," that is, having to do not with political issues but with the private settling of accounts on such matters as debt, property, and sexual and marital issues, robberies, barroom brawls, and family violence. As a result, homicides in 1986 averaged between 2.17 and 6.46 per day in Cali and between 5.77 and 9.70 in Medellín.[26] In Puerto Boyacá, in July 1991, the death-squad leader Henry de Jesús Pérez was assassinated during a religious ceremony. Pérez had been indicted and convicted for the massacre of campesinos in the Urabá banana zone, and when the local head of the national police was asked why this convicted murderer had not been arrested he replied in effect that he had received no orders to do so. A Colombian sociologist, expert on the military and the police, had a simpler explanation: The Pérez death squad was more numerous and better armed than the local contingent of the police.[27]

Similarly, in the Minero River basin, in the western part of the department of Boyacá, where 80 percent of the emeralds of Colombia are produced and there is a long tradition of violence, the money made in emeralds was being transferred to the cultivation, processing, and marketing of coca. According to the Commission for the Study of the Violence,

In this context, the state has not acted as an arbiter of the different economic and political interests at play. It is thus not possible for these interests to express themselves thoroughly through legal channels. The state . . . has rather seemed to be an institutional entity of very low legitimacy, beside which, or in relation with which, organized groups operate, taking over state functions (such as providing security and justice). A social world thus is erected where multiple systems of law and justice reign, a world where official institutional government and the noninstitutional coexist.[28]

According to the Colombian government itself, at least 80 percent of the crimes in the country went unreported, and of those reported only 10 percent led to indictments and convictions. Amnesty International stated in November 1989 that 2,500 Colombians had been executed "extrajuridically" during the previous eighteen months. In January 1990 the government reported that 380 Colombians were being held by kidnappers, including those held by drug dealers, guerrillas, and common criminals.[29] Homicide had become the leading cause of death in Colombia. At the same time, evidence suggested that the Colombian government controlled less and less of the territory outside of the major cities. One study indicated that the "self-defense" groups of Magdalena Medio were performing most of the functions of government, including justice, education, and health care,[30] and the indication was that the FARC did the same thing in the remote areas of recent colonization in the Amazon area of the country.[31] In other areas the government had a presence but shared functions with the paramilitaries.

Experts disagree over the causes of the high level of criminality in Colombia. Some consider the basic problem to be a lack of police personnel, while others suggest that it is a mistaken emphasis on guerrilla- and drug-related violence instead of common crime, rapid urbanization, the absence of a tradition of peaceful conflict resolution, or the inequities of the Colombian economic system. What is certain is that there is a palpable sense of insecurity in the country's major cities.

Conclusion

Since the end of the National Front, Colombia has approximated a "democratic" system, at least in the manner of choosing its chief executive, but the compromise that this system requires has perpetuated the immobilism of earlier times. The Barco years demonstrated that Colombian politicians were not prepared for partisan government, especially when drug traffickers, guerrillas, and paramilitaries were challenging the entire system. The "Top 10" stories of Semana's first ten years of publication graphically depict the state of Colombia between 1982 and 1992: (1) Belisario Betancur elected president; (2) Gabriel García Márquez receives Nobel Prize for Literature; (3) the assassination of Rodrigo Lara; (4) the meeting of Alfonso López with Pablo Escobar and the Ochoa brothers in Panama; (5) the M-19 occupation of the Palacio de Justicia and the response of the military; (6)

Former President César Gaviria, 1990–1994; Secretary General of the Organization of American States, 1994–present (Photo courtesy of the Organization of American States.)

the attempt to find and arrest Pablo Escobar; (7) the assassination of Luis Carlos Galá; (8) the capture and extradition of Carlos Lehder; (9) the Santodomingo case (in which a leading investor under indictment for fraud mysteriously disappeared from prison and the country); (10) the new right, led by President César Gaviria.[32] The *Semana* list is dominated by headlines related to violence.

Debates continue in Colombia over what should be done to end the violence. Some saw Gaviria's deal with Escobar as a capitulation to terror; others point out

that the bloodiest year in history has been followed by fewer deaths from drug-related bombings. Some argue that the government should not negotiate with kidnappers and killers; other hold that negotiating with guerrillas is appropriate, because their violence is principled, but negotiating with drug traffickers is not,
since theirs is about money. Still others argue that a strong government should
punish murderers no matter what their motivations. The situation calls to mind
Simón Bolívar's characterization of Nueva Granada as a "debating society." One
product of this debate was a demand for a change of the constitution—for more
democracy as a way out of the imbroglio.

Notes

1. Luís Alberto Restrepo, "The Crisis of the Current Political Regime and Its Possible
Outcomes," in Berquist, Peñaranda, and Sánchez, *Violence in Colombia,* 185.

2. Mario Latorre, quoted in *El Espectador* (Bogotá), August 24, 1986.

3. The title of this chapter on the period 1974–1994 is suggested by Francisco Leal
Buitrago and León Zamosc (eds.), *Al filo del caos: Crisis política en la Colombia de los años
80* (Bogotá: Tercer Mundo Editores, 1990). Alternative descriptions of the period include
"entering the abyss," in the words of former President Misael Pastrana (*Miami Herald,* June
12, 1988), and "getting screwed up," as in *En Qué momento se jodió Colombia* (Bogotá:
Editorial Oveja Negra, 1990).

4. Daniel L. Premo, "The Armed Forces and Colombian Politics: In Search of a
Mission," mimeographed (Chestertown, Md.: Washington College, 1981); John Agudelo
Villa, president of Betancur's Peace Commission, quoted in *El Espectador* (Bogotá),
October 14, 1986; confidential interview with a member of the executive branch, July 21,
1992.

5. Eduardo Pizarro, "Revolutionary Guerrilla Groups in Colombia," Berquist,
Peñaranda, and Sánchez, *Violence in Colombia,* 177.

6. Ibid., 180–181.

7. Ibid., 179.

8. Ibid., 182–183.

9. Ibid., 185.

10. *El Tiempo* (Bogotá), March 24, 1981; *El Espectador* (Bogotá), May 23, 1982.

11. *El Espectador* (Bogotá), November 21, 1982.

12. *El Espectador* (Bogotá), May 27, 1984.

13. *Cromos* (Bogotá), July 19, 1985, my translation.

14. Bruce Bagley, "Colombia and The War on Drugs," *Foreign Affairs* 67 (1988):73–74.

15. Ibid., 75–76.

16. Richard B. Craig, "Domestic Implications of Illicit Drug Cultivation, Processing,
and Trafficking in Colombia," paper presented at the U.S. State Department Conference on
Colombia, Washington, D.C., November 9, 1981, 4–5.

17. Ibid.

18. *Latin America Weekly Report,* January 8, 1982.

19. *El Espectador* (Bogotá), July 31, 1988, my translation.

20. *Semana,* October 2–9, 1990.

21. *Semana,* July 31–August 7, 1990.

22. *Semana,* August 25–September 1, 1992, 25.

23. Jorge Orlando Melo, "Los paramilitares y su impacto sobre la política," in Francisco Leal Buitrago and León Zamosc, *Al filo del caos: Crisis política en la Colombia de los años 80* (Bogotá: Tercer Mundo Editores, 1990), 493.

24. Pizarro, "Revolutionary Guerrilla Groups," 189–190.

25. Confidential interviews with members of the executive branch, Bogotá, July 21, 1992; July 22, 1992.

26. Alvaro Camacho, "Public and Private Dimensions of Urban Violence in Colombia," in Berquist, Peñaranda, and Sánchez, *Violence in Colombia,* 241–242.

27. Confidential interview with a Colombian sociologist, July 18, 1991.

28. Commission for the Study of the Violence, "Organized Violence," in Berquist, Peñaranda, and Sánchez, *Violence in Colombia,* 264.

29. *El Espectador* (Bogotá), January 14, 1990.

30. Carlos Medina Gallego, *Autodefensas, paramilitares y narcotráfico en Colombia* (Bogotá: Editorial Documentos Periodísticos, 1990), 219–242.

31. Confidential interview with a Colombian sociologist, July 27, 1992.

32. *Semana,* May 12–19, 1992, 50–51.

5

GOVERNMENT AND POLITICS

AS IN MANY LATIN AMERICAN countries, in Colombia constitutions are not always followed to the letter and laws are not always enforced, either for lack of bureaucratic capacity to do so or because this was never the intention. This disparity between the formal and informal exists at all levels of law, leading some Colombian leaders to say in the late 1980s that the problem was not the constitution but the inability to enforce existing law. Yet there were persistent calls for institutional change, and in 1988 constitutional reform was initiated with its consideration by the two houses of Congress. After two sessions, however, no reform was proposed.

When all the politicians thought that the issue was dead, university students entered the process, calling for voters to deposit an extra ballot in the March 1990 congressional elections as an indication that they wanted a constituent assembly to produce a new constitution. More than a million such ballots were deposited. After the Supreme Court ruled that this was an acceptable way of changing the 1886 Constitution, on May 27, 1990 (the day of the presidential election), Colombian voters voted yes or no on this question: "In order to fortify participatory democracy, do you vote for the convocation of a constituent assembly with representation of social, political, and regional forces, integrated democratically and popularly, to reform the Constitution of Colombia?" There were 4,991,887 affirmative votes, while 226,451 voted no.[1]

In late July 1990 President-elect Gaviria proposed the following ten topics for consideration by the Constituent Assembly:

1. Congressional reform, including different functions for the two houses, a new system of elections, and a national electoral district for guerrilla groups observing truces.
2. Changes in the justice system, including plea bargaining, pardon by judges, the use of plural judges in some cases, and the protection of the identity of judges and witnesses.
3. Democratization of the public administration system so that interested parties could make their opinions known before administrative decisions were made.
4. More express enumeration and protection of human rights.
5. Statutes to regulate political parties and opposition, including financial control.
6. Redistribution of governmental rights to legislative and executive leaders at the departmental and municipal levels.
7. Mechanisms to give citizens more rights to participate in the political, social, economic, administrative, and cultural aspects of the nation, including the referendum.
8. Changes of the state of siege, with more precise specifications for the transitory, abnormal situation and with various stages according to the nature of the disruption of public order.
9. Increased involvement of the Congress in the economic planning process and in investment programs.
10. Giving the Congress the power to carry out investigations in its oversight control of the executive.

The president made it clear, however, that the reforms were a means to an end: "Obviously it would be simplistic to pretend that with reforms the violence and terrorism will disappear immediately. It [constitutional reform] is a matter of finding more efficacious instruments for confronting them."[2]

The Supreme Court later ruled that while the election of a constituent assembly was constitutional, limiting the assembly to Gaviria's ten points was not. The elections held on December 6, 1990, gave twenty-five seats to the Liberal party, nineteen to the Alianza Democrática M-19, eleven to the Movimiento de Salvación Nacional, five to the Partido Conservador, four to the Independent Conservatives, and eight to the Independents. The assembly began its sessions on February 5, 1991, and the new constitution was promulgated on July 4, 1991.

The Executive Branch

The executive branch is the strongest branch of government, and the president is the person with the most power. This concentration of power was an important target of the framers of the new constitution. The president is elected for a four-year term and is not eligible for reelection (Constitution of 1991; the 1886

Constitution prohibited only *immediate* reelection). While under the 1886 Constitution only a plurality was needed for election, under the new constitution a majority is required. There will be two electoral rounds if no one receives a majority in the first. Under the old constitution there was no vice president; rather, a designate (*designado*), elected for a two-year term by the Congress, took over upon the death, resignation, or temporary incapacitation of the president and, on occasion, when the president left the country. Under the new formula a vice president is to be elected with the president, although they do not have to be from the same party.

Under the Constitution of 1886, the formal powers of the president were impressive. He named and removed (without congressional concurrence) cabinet officials, heads of government agencies, governors of the departments, and other public officials. Under the new constitution governors are elected; the Congress can remove a cabinet official by a vote of censure. Both constitutions charge the president with maintaining national security, declaring war (with the permission of the Senate, unless foreign aggression makes such impossible), and negotiating foreign treaties. He can direct war operations, when necessary, as the commander of the armed forces. His formal powers in the day-to-day workings of the government are sweeping, including conferring military degrees and directing the military; collecting taxes; regulating, directing, and inspecting national public education; negotiating contracts for public works; organizing public credit; exercising the inspection of banks and corporations; and preserving public order.

As if the above powers and others that the constitution lists were not impressive enough, under the 1886 Constitution the president, confronting international war or internal disturbances, could declare a "state of siege." All cabinet ministers had to approve this declaration (but of course all were named by, and could be removed by, the chief executive). During the state of siege the president ruled by decree (which also had to be approved by all the ministers). These decrees could not overturn existing laws but could suspend them. Congress continued to meet as it normally would, and all decrees promulgated had to be sent the following day to the Supreme Court, which could declare them unconstitutional.

The Constitution of 1991, recognizing that the country in the past four decades had been under a state of siege more often than not, greatly limited the president's powers. He now can decree a "state of internal commotion," but it can only last for ninety days in a calendar year, extendable for only another ninety through a vote of the Senate. Further, according to the Constitution of 1886 as amended in the 1970s, in the case of economic crisis the president could declare a "state of emergency." This was similar to the state of siege, but with the stipulation that the decrees issued could deal only with the specific situation that led to the declaration. It could last a maximum of ninety days a year. The Constitution of 1991 now allows the president to declare a state of emergency not only in the case of economic problems but also when there are ecological or social difficulties "that constitute a grave public calamity." The state of emergency can be declared for only thirty days at a time and only ninety days per calendar year.

These provisions of the Constitution are extremely important for understanding Colombian politics since 1949. For example, the state of siege declared near the end of the López Michelsen administration was still in force when Julio César Turbay became president in August 1978. The following month Turbay, using his decree power, promulgated a Security Statute that remained in force until he rescinded it in July 1982. A response to general insecurity, crime, terrorism, and kidnapping, the statute established longer prison sentences for crimes such as kidnapping, leadership and membership in subversive bands, disruption of public order, bribery, inciting to riot, illegally occupying public offices, and manufacturing, distributing, transporting, and carrying firearms, ammunitions, or explosives. Further, it prohibited broadcasting by television or radio any declaration, communiqué, or commentary about public order, illegal strikes, or any other news story that might incite disorder. Individuals arrested for these crimes (other than the broadcasting and firearms provisions) were tried by courts-martial.

While these stipulations were far-reaching, the Supreme Court and the Congress constrained them to a degree. The Supreme Court declared certain parts of the statute unconstitutional (for example, the provision that "subversive propaganda" could not be distributed in government offices) and in 1981 ruled that the new legal code passed by the Congress the previous year superseded the prison sentences established by the statute. Yet neither governmental branch addressed the basic questions of courts-martial and the absence of the right to bail.

In addition to the decree power during states of siege, a Colombian president had the power to promulgate regulations (*decretos reglamentarios*) interpreting the laws passed by the Congress. He had to be careful, however, not to change those laws; any Colombian could initiate a suit that might lead to the Supreme Court's overturning all or part of such a regulatory decree.

As impressive as these formal powers are, whether a particular president is a shaper of policy or merely a "chief clerk" depends on a variety of factors. In the first place, no one person *could do* everything that the president *has the power to do*—especially when ceremonial duties all over the country are added to the powers already enumerated. By necessity, then, some power has to be delegated to cabinet ministers. Other powers, by law, have been given to decentralized institutes (*institutos descentralizados*)—agencies of the executive branch more or less under the supervision of the various ministries.

The president's cabinet was by law, between 1958 and 1991, a coalition one. As we have seen, only Virgilio Barco did not follow this rule. This sometimes meant that a politician who was in opposition to legislation proposed by the president one year might be in the cabinet the next. For example, in 1979 Senator Felio Andrade led the opposition to the Turbay administration's Coal Law. In 1980–1981, Andrade was minister of justice in the Turbay cabinet. The shifting sands of coalition formation placed limits on the president's power.

The relationship between the president and the cabinet was a matter of controversy. An individual president, if he had the inclination, could at times personally (or along with a few ministers) make policy changes. Thus, it is said, Carlos Lleras

Restrepo was able to force a renegotiation of oil contracts in the Putumayo region despite the recalcitrance of the multinationals.[3] Others stressed that the president had a term much longer than the ministers'. Alfonso López, for example, had five ministers of mines and energy in four years and Turbay three in his first three. As one former minister said, "This is just one of the givens of Colombian politics; you have to work within it."[4] What is not completely clear, however, is whether this ministerial turnover was a result of policy disagreements or of other factors such as the requirements of coalition formation and the desire of ministers to move on to elected political office. Some observers suggested that although "minor" ministers came and went with great rapidity there was stability in the two "superministers"–the minister of the treasury and the minister of defense.[5] Further, some of the turnover involved individuals' shifting from one high-level post to another. It was not a sign of significant change, for example, when Jaime García Parra shifted from minister of mines to minister of the treasury.

Even if the president and the ministers agreed on policy within an area, there were societal constraints on their power. They could not make public policy unilaterally if the interests of organized economic groups such as the producers' associations and the unions were involved and if the policy changes had to be made through legislation by Congress. At times ministers (with or without presidential approval) apparently had considerable "initiative space,"[6] but how much of this initiative space was "decision space" depended on the strength of the affected parties. Further potential constraints on the executive's power came from within the executive branch itself: from the bureaucracy, the decentralized institutes, the National Planning Department (Departamento Nacional de Planeación, DNP), and the National Council of Economic and Social Policy (Consejo Nacional de Política Económica y Social, CONPES).

The growth of the Colombian bureaucracy in recent decades has been almost exponential. As early as the Liberal hegemony of 1940–1946, the bureaucracy began growing as the state took on more responsibilities. The first decentralized institute was founded during the Santos administration. The National Front put even more emphasis on government's role in the society and the economy, and the rate of growth increased. Indeed, some even argue that parity was simply a matter of adding new bureaucrats rather than firing any of the existing ones. Bureaucratic jobs were much sought after. Although salaries were not high, the jobs were white-collar and carried the prestige of the "mental sector." Since at most 15 percent of bureaucrats were part of the civil service, party or factional loyalty was more important than technical expertise in obtaining positions. Article 120 ensured the second party "adequate and equitable" participation, but since few bureaucrats were fired when governing coalitions changed, the group was poorly paid and poorly treated.

The earliest of the decentralized institutes (Table 5.1), the Industrial Promotion Institute (Instituto de Fomento Industrial, IFI), was established in 1940. The institutes were "under the tutelage" of a ministry, which meant that the respective minister was usually a member of the board of directors of the institute and hence

TABLE 5.1   Major Decentralized Institutes, 1990

Ministry	Institute	Function
Public Works and	INTRA	Transportation
Transportation	COLPUERTOS	Ports
	FFCC	Railroads
Communications	ADPOSTAL	Mail
	TELECOM	Telephone, telegraph
	INRAVISION	Television
Education	COLCIENCIAS	Science
	COLCULTURAS	Culture
	COLDEPORTES	Sports
	ICFES	University education
Economic Development	INCOMEX	Foreign commerce
	ICT	Housing credit
	PROEXPO	Exports
	IFI	Industrial promotion
Mines and Energy	INGEOMINAS	Geological investigations
	ICEL	Electricity
	ECOMINAS	Mines
	ECOPETROL	Petroleum
	CARBOCOL	Coal
Labor and Social	ICBF	Welfare
Security	ICSS	Social Security
	SENA	Technical education
Agriculture	INCORA	Agrarian reform
	INDERENA	Renewable resources, environment
	HIMAT	Water resources, meteorology
	Caja Agraria	Credit
	Banco Ganadero	Credit
Treasury and Public	Banco Central	Mortgages
Credit	Hipotecario	
	Banco de la	Central bank
	República	

played a role in policy. Yet as ministers came and went the institutes remained. For example, while there were eight ministers of mines between 1974 and 1982, the Colombian Petroleum Enterprise (Empresa Colombiana de Petróleos, ECOPETROL), founded in 1951, had two directors. Indeed, ECOPETROL was said to have considerable independence in its internal policy.[7] (The minister of mines and the president of course played important roles in naming the director of ECOPETROL.) During the Turbay years it was reported that the head of ECOPETROL was the son of a friend of the president and that he had received the position over other presumably more able candidates nominated by the ministers of mines and the treasury. But the staffs of the institutes did tend to be less a part of the political-patronage game than their counterparts in the bureaucracy directly under the ministries. They also were paid higher salaries than the regular bureaucrats (although not so high that private business—both Colombian and multinational—could not offer them better).

The institutes in fact received more of the national budget each year than the ministries did and had more independence in policymaking. In the absence of a forceful minister (which is to say, most of the time) they were likely to carry out their programs without concern about the overall national interest and without coordination with other institutes.

For this reason, governments since the National Front have sought a way of coordinating policy through what today are called the DNP and the CONPES. The first attempt was in 1958, when a National Council of Economic Policy and Planning was established. Made up of the president and four additional members (two named by the president, one by the Senate, and one by the Chamber of Deputies), this council was to study and coordinate economic policies, project general development plans, and present governmental intentions to the private sector.[8] A second attempt, in 1963, modified the functions of this council to concentrate on plan approval and implementation. Its membership included the president (chairman), the ministers of the treasury, development, agriculture, and public works, the head of the planning department, the manager of the Banco de la República, and the manager of the National Federation of Coffee Growers (Federación Nacional de Cafeteros, FEDECAFE). Finally, in 1968 the council was expanded and given its current name: Added were the ministers of foreign relations and labor and the director of the Colombian Institute of Foreign Commerce (Instituto Colombiano de Comercio Exterior, INCOMEX). Moreover, representatives of technical public organizations were permitted to attend council meetings on the invitation of the president. The council was assigned four basic functions: to recommend general economic policies as guides for plans, to study and evaluate plans submitted by the DNP, to study periodic reports prepared by the DNP's secretary general, and to coordinate the economic policies and activities of the state.

By 1968 the DNP had evolved to the point of having a permanent staff. The reform of that year gave it impressive powers (at least on paper): to develop norms for the establishment and operation of departmental, municipal, and other sectoral offices, provide technical assistance to these offices, prepare development plans and present them to the CONPES, evaluate and seek adjustments during plan implementation, study sectoral, regional, and local plans and incorporate them into general development plans, make proposals regarding economic policies and submit special studies to the CONPES, coordinate the preparation of plans with other public institutions, and submit to the president and the Congress reports on plan execution.

If the DNP and the CONPES worked as they are supposed to, they would ensure rationality in planning and continuity from one presidency to the next and constrain the power of any president. Yet neither organization has been an effective coordinator. For one thing, the commitment to planning has varied from one presidency to another; politically—in a very patronage-oriented administration such as that of Turbay—it was easier to allow the decentralized institutes to go their own way. For another, DNP officials tend to have short tenures in office, often being hired away by private businesses that can offer better salaries. It seems reasonable to conclude that the Colombian system—which is supposed to be one of "indicative planning" for the private sector and obligatory planning for the public one—is more one of indicative planning for the public sector and no planning at all for the private one. Lack of coordination is a chronic problem in the public sector, and it is likely to continue.

The Congress and the Supreme Court

Although secondary in power, both the Congress and the Supreme Court have had some authority. The Congress has been an arena for modifying or blocking legislation, but few laws of any importance have originated there.

The Legislative Branch

Under the Constitution of 1886 the electoral district for the Congress was the department. Each department has two senators, plus an additional one for each 200,000 inhabitants, and two representatives in the Chamber of Deputies, plus an additional one for each 100,000 inhabitants. Terms in both houses were and remain four years. The Constitution of 1991 left the lower house based on departments, although its size was reduced. The hundred-member Senate, however, is elected by a national constituency, thus favoring minor parties.

The electoral system used for both houses is a proportional-representation list system, in which voters choose a complete list. If a list has the right to two senators (for example), the first two on the list are elected. Further, under the Constitution of 1886 both members (*principales*) and alternates (*suplentes*) were elected. If any member decided not to attend the Congress, the first alternate took his or her place. To complicate matters, this particular variant of the list system (like the former *ley del lema* in Uruguay) encourages multiple lists, and if any list receives less than half of the electoral quotient (defined as the total number of votes divided by the number of seats) its votes are assigned to the list with the same label that received the most votes. The Constitution of 1991 did away with alternates; now if an elected member of either house cannot attend Congress, he or she is replaced by the first person on the list who was not awarded a seat on the basis of the number of votes.

As a result of these structures (engineered, no doubt, because of the factionalism of Colombian politics), the Congress was the *país político* par excellence. In the 1980s one found in it Turbay Liberals, Lleras Liberals, adherents of Galán's New Liberalism, Gómez Conservatives, Betancur Conservatives, Pastrana Conservatives, members of ANAPO, Unión Patriótica members, Communists, and others. Although Colombia's was generally considered a two-party system, the Congress operated with more of a multiparty one. On any issue the natural leaders of the factions took the lead, and those who hoped that loyalty would help them achieve a high position (*renglón*) on the list the next time followed. Coalitions tended to be transitory. The case of coal policy in the early 1980s is instructive. In 1979 the Turbay Liberals and the Pastrana Conservatives favored the Coal Law, and the opposition was led by the Gómez conservatives; in 1981 the Lleras Liberals and Unionist Conservatives (albeit with mixed signals) opposed the Turbay Liberals and the Gómez Conservatives. It is little wonder that the Congress was less and less a policymaking branch. The 1991 Constitution aimed to change this.

The 1968 constitutional reform had explicitly taken power from the Congress. Under it the president could declare any initiative to be "urgent," hence giving the Congress only thirty days to defeat it, and all economic bills had to originate in the administration. The major contribution to planning by the Congress was to be the Plan Commission (Comisión del Plan), a bicameral body that met for the first time thirteen years after it was established. The 1991 Constitution, in contrast, was intended to ensure the election of more responsible members of Congress and to give it more power. Under the 1886 Constitution, individual politicians could hold posts in all three levels of legislatures at the same time: Congress, the departmental assembly, and the municipal council. The Congress typically ground to a halt when the assemblies began their short sessions. Further, the lack of a residency requirement might mean that a politician represented one area of the country in the Congress, served on the council of a city, and was a member of the assembly in yet another area of the country. This lack of a residency requirement also applied to the appointive positions of governor and mayor. The 1991 Constitution made it impossible to serve in more than one legislative body at a time.

Under the Constitution of 1886, the Congress convened on July 20 each year and had regular sessions of 150 days. If its work was not finished, at the end of this period presidents called extraordinary sessions during which only executive proposals could be considered. Ministers were questioned on the floor of the two houses and could be cited if they failed to attend. The reformers of 1991 increased the yearly sessions to two, the first from July 20 to December 16 and the second from March 16 to June 20. Displeasure with the old structure was so intense the Constituent Assembly deposed the Congress elected under the 1886 Constitution in 1990, establishing that there would be new elections in October 1991.

The Judicial Branch

Under the Constitution of 1886 the judicial branch was headed by a supreme court. It had a varying number of members (as established by law) elected to eight-year terms by the court itself. The court ruled on the legality of presidential decrees. It also judged officials who had been impeached by the Senate and determined the constitutionality of laws passed by the Congress. Perhaps the most notable exercise of power by the Supreme Court in recent years was the October 1981 declaration that the Constitutional reform of 1979 (which President Turbay had called the most important reform of the century) was unconstitutional. This decision was based on procedural irregularities during the 1979 sessions of the Congress. The Turbay administration reacted angrily, accusing the court of making the decision on political grounds and arguing that such a decision required a three-fifths vote.[9] In the end, the court's ruling stood.

Because the failure of the justice system to deal with recent violence was one of the major reasons for the Constituent Assembly of 1991, the new constitution included the following major changes: While the Supreme Court will remain preeminent in ordinary law and the Council of State in administrative disputes, a new Constitutional Court will be "in charge of guarding the integrity and supremacy of the Constitution." The way has been opened for the creation of justices of the peace to handle individual disputes. A national prosecutor, elected for a four-year term by the Supreme Court, will be charged with the investigation of crimes, indictments, and coordination of the national investigative bodies for these purposes. (Previous to this change, as in most Latin American countries, judges were responsible for investigating as well as hearing cases.) Finally, a Superior Council has been set up to administer the judiciary.

It is perhaps too soon to know if these changes will have the intended effects. Early evidence is that the national prosecutor's office is processing 50 percent more cases a year than the previous system, but there is still much room for improvement.

Regional and Local Government

Colombia is divided into twenty-seven departments, and each has a governor. Under the 1886 Constitution governors were named and removed by the president; the 1991 Constitution makes governorships elective. Each department also has a departmental assembly, elected through a proportional-representation system similar to that for the Congress. The assembly is secondary in power to the governor.

Each of the more than 1,000 *municipios* has a mayor, before 1988 named by the governor (with the exception of the mayor of Bogotá, who was named by the president) and since 1988 elected for a two-year term without the possibility of immediate reelection. Each *municipio* also has a council elected through the proportional-representation list system. The council is secondary in power to the mayor.

Under the Constitution of 1886 both departments and *municipios* were weak in comparison with the national government. Although there were some bureaucracies at those levels, most Colombian bureaucrats were part of the national government. Tax revenues for the department and *municipio* governments were limited. Departments received most of their revenues from their liquor monopolies and lotteries; municipalities increasingly used property taxes (and for some time had been collecting fees for the provision of municipal services such as garbage removal and water). One of the goals of the 1991 Constitution was to strengthen local and regional government. To that end, tax revenues collected by the national government were to be shared with them, increasing from a minimum of 14 percent in 1993 to 22 percent in 2002.

Parties and Interest Groups

Organized groups in Colombian society tend to be most effective at the upper socioeconomic levels of society. Labor is less well organized and the poor hardly at all. The government retains the right to withhold the legal recognition without which no group can legally exist. The Colombian state therefore does not approach the organic model—with all the major sectors of society organized by a single government-recognized group—as closely as do Brazil and Mexico.

Political Parties

Political parties in Colombia have always been elitist instruments of control. Leadership has almost always come from the highest socioeconomic groups, whether or not one wished to call them an oligarchy as the Colombians do. Whereas some point to presidents of humble origins such as Marco Fidel Suárez, Conservative president during the 1920s, who was born in a grass hut, the illegitimate son of a washerwoman, they do not mention that by the time his political career began he had married into a traditional family.[10] The myth that anyone can be president gained apparent substantiation from the 1982 election of Belisario Betancur (one of twenty-two children of an illiterate peasant), but the fact of elite control of the parties remains. Although parties have created effective linkages from the top down, they have failed at interest aggregation. In seeking to incorporate emergent social groups, parties may promise fulfillment of some of the aspirations of those groups, but the goal is to capture and control them.

For the past thirty years, the real conflicts in elite politics have been between the various factions of the two parties. These factional disputes—with name-calling and accusations—take up more space in the major Bogotá newspapers than the traditional Liberal-Conservative conflicts. In a series of lectures given by the presidential "precandidates" (those pursuing the nomination of their party conventions) in 1981 at the Universidad de los Andes in Bogotá, two of the three said that there were no longer any ideological differences between the two parties. The Conservative, Belisario Betancur, put it most poetically: "The difference is that the color of the Conservative party is blue, the color of the Virgin Mary. The Liberal color is red, color of the Sacred Heart of Jesus."[11]

Only three factions have in the past decade attempted to present different ideological programs. The first of these, the New Liberalism of Luis Carlos Galán and others, in June 1981 announced a program including the following major points:

- radical transformation of the Congress
- regulation and publication of candidates' financial resources
- the "relief" (*relevo*) of the political oligarchy that dominated the Congress
- intervention of the state in the growth of the large cities
- defense of human rights
- control of monopolies and oligopolies
- revision of all contracts in petroleum, coal, uranium, and other natural resources
- reorganization of the state for the defense of national sovereignty in the face of the financial and technological power of large foreign companies
- cultural identity and the recovery and diffusion of "the values that explain the national conscience"
- defense of the rights of indigenous populations
- television reform
- support of the spirit of progressive unionism.[12]

The other two programs came from within the Conservative party. The Movimiento de Salvación Nacional (Movement of National Salvation), led by Conservative warhorse Alvaro Gómez Hurtado, was established to support Gómez's 1990 presidential campaign and later used to elect members of the Constituent Assembly and five senators in the 1991 election. Its ideology was an "Agreement on the Fundamental," mostly a law-and-order platform. The Nueva Fuerza Democrática (New Democratic Force), set up by Andrés Pastrana (son of former president Misael Pastrana and the first elected mayor of Bogotá), elected nine members of the Senate in 1991 and was a bipartisan attempt to bring change to Colombia. These two splinter groups were led by individuals with longstanding family ties to the party and represent the deep split in the party going back to Laureano Gómez (father of Alvaro) and Mariano Ospina Pérez, replaced in the 1970s by Misael Pastrana (father of Andrés).

Ten years ago some argued that the party elites were in the process of realignment. It was suggested that new political parties or more permanent coalitions between progressive Liberals (Galán) and Conservatives (Betancur) might emerge from the process. In this regard, the 1982 presidential campaign is instructive. After the last-minute entry of Alfonso López Michelsen as a precandidate and his capture of the Liberal nomination, Luis Carlos Galán announced his candidacy without the party's imprimatur and quickly received the endorsement of Carlos Lleras and of a leading Bogotá daily, *El Espectador*. This Liberal behavior, reminiscent of the 1946 election, allowed the Conservatives to offer a single candidate, Belisario Betancur, for the May 30 election. The Liberals were unable to reach an agreement that the congressional elections (held in March) would serve as a kind of "primary," even though such an agreement had been reached in 1978 in similar circumstances. Nor did a Liberal candidate drop out after the congressional elections, even though the congressional lists identified with López won 46 percent of the vote while the Galán lists won only 11 percent. In the end, there were three candidates in the May elections. The Liberal party received a majority of the votes, but they were split between López (40 percent) and Galán (12 percent). Betancur won the presidency with 47 percent of the more than 7 million votes cast, becoming the first Conservative to be elected in a competitive election between the two traditional parties since Mariano Ospina in 1946 (when again there were two Liberal candidates).

Public-opinion surveys in the 1980s showed that only 64 percent of respondents in Bogotá identified with one of the two traditional parties in 1978 (46 percent Liberal and 18 percent Conservative), as compared with 73 percent in 1974 and 80 percent in 1970.[13] In the 1982 presidential election, for example, no doubt many who considered themselves "Liberals" voted for the Conservative Betancur, even though López made some attempts at "waving the bloody flag" of party loyalty. This weakening of party identification can perhaps be attributed to urbanization and rapid population growth. By the 1980s Colombians were primarily urban and therefore had neither the traditional patron-client relationships nor the problems on which party loyalty had been based. Further, almost half of the Colombians living in the 1980s had never experienced partisan violence.

By 1991 there remained little doubt: The Liberal party was still clearly the majority party in Colombia, and the Conservatives were weak and fragmented. It is significant that neither Gómez's National Salvation Movement nor Pastrana's New Democratic Force was advertised as a Conservative movement. Yet the situation was still in flux. Gómez supported Pastrana in the presidential election, while in the congressional elections chaos prevailed. The Liberal strategy, first used in the 1991 congressional elections, was one of a "wasp swarm," the metaphor referring to getting all the major regional leaders to head Liberal lists for the two houses of Congress. In the 1994 congressional elections *all* of the parties adopted this strategy. For the hundred-member Senate, elected from a national constituency, members were elected from ninety-eight different lists; only two lists elected two senators each. One Colombian sociologist commented,

President Ernesto Samper, 1994–1998 (Photo courtesy of the
Organization of American States.)

Given this situation, it's my opinion that we no longer have political parties. Or
maybe we have two parties with no discipline, or maybe three, although since the
AD-M19 did not elect a single senator it's hard to count them. Or maybe we have
ninety-eight parties in the Senate. But what's clear is that the "wasp swarm" strategy
was the cause of the current situation, with leaders approving all kinds of lists so that
they could later say their party had won so many seats.[14]

No doubt the most important of the smaller parties today is the AD-M19,
which, as we have seen, was founded when the M-19 turned in its weapons in
1989. Its presidential candidate, Antonio Navarro, not only finished third in the
presidential election with 12.5 percent of the vote but was one of the three copres-
idents of the 1991 Constituent Assembly. This post was due to the AD-M19's having the list that received the most votes and being the second-largest group in the
assembly (after the Liberals), with nineteen seats. The AD-M19 won nine seats in

the Senate in the 1991 elections but none in 1994. It is basically a coalition of former M-19 members, members of other demobilized guerrilla groups (especially
the EPL), and others who see this as a better solution for the country's problems
than the traditional parties. Its electoral failure in 1994 was largely due to leadership splits.

The oldest minor party is the Colombian Communist Party (Partido Comunista Colombiano, PCC), which has existed for over sixty years. Although at
times it has been illegal, today it offers candidates and occasionally elects them.
The Unión Patriótica (UP), set up by the FARC during its truce with the Betancur
government, has been supported by the PCC and has similar programs. The UP
has seen one of its presidential candidates assassinated and reported in 1991 that
over 1,000 of its members had been killed in three years. Other radical parties
have generally been unable to agree on a single presidential candidate and never
account for more than 10 percent, and in 1982 Gerardo Molina, a coalition candidate of the Communists and various radical groups, received only 1 percent.

In the Constituent Assembly election of 1990 and the congressional ones of
1991, the AD-M19 seemed to have broken the historical pattern of the fragmenta-
tion and unpopularity with voters of the left. Since the 1994 elections, however, it
still seems safest to conclude that the Liberals will continue to win presidential
and dominate congressional elections.

Trade Associations

Trade associations (*gremios*) have joined the traditional parties as the most powerful forces in Colombia since the beginning of the National Front. Today some
even suggest that they are more important than the parties.[15] Probably the most
powerful of these is the National Association of Industrialists (Asociación
Nacional de Industriales, ANDI), which includes not only the large industrialists
but also firms in agribusiness, insurance, finance, and commerce. Founded in
1944, ANDI is the leading advocate of free enterprise in Colombia and has important roots in the industrialist sector of Medellín. It is powerful because of its
wealth and social prestige, the overlapping of its membership with that of the
government, and the fact that industrialization had been a major goal of almost
every Colombian president of the past half-century. ANDI tends to oppose anything that might negatively affect the private sector but has historically supported
the government against radical opposition.

Other major producer associations are shown in Table 5.2. All come from the
upper sector, and all seek to maintain the status quo. Most elements of the private
sector have been antimilitary, and some of these associations were important in
the 1957 fall of Rojas Pinilla. Although they have sometimes disagreed with the
policy of a government, they have supported the political regime. They tend to re-
act to government policy rather than initiating policy. With the growth of the executive branch—both in the ministries and the decentralized institutes—the associations have developed strong ties with that branch. This does not mean,

TABLE 5.2   Major Producer Associations, 1994

Sector	Association
Industry (large)	ANDI
Industry (small and medium)	ACOPI
Agriculture	SAC
Coffee	FEDECAFE
Livestock Raisers	FEDEGAN
Commerce	FENALCO
Commerce	CONFECAMARAS
Banking	ASOBANCARIA
Banking and Finance	ANIF
Construction	CAMACOL
Insurance	FASECOLDA

however, that they will not use connections within the Congress if this is a more effective way of blocking governmental policy.

FEDECAFE, founded in 1927, is open to anyone interested in developing the coffee industry but is dominated by the large coffee growers. It collects various taxes on coffee and has invested its wealth in banks and shipping. Given the importance of coffee to economic policy, it has a close relationship with the government. Nowhere else in Latin America would a private organization be allowed to do what FEDECAFE does; the government would do it directly.[16]

With the lack of differentiation of the political parties and their factions, interest articulation and aggregation have increasingly fallen to the trade associations (which have made efforts to be bipartisan) and to the church and the military. For example, in April 1981 the Frente Gremial, composed of the presidents of ANDI, the Colombian Chamber of Construction (Cámara Colombiana de Construcción, CAMACOL), the Colombian Federation of Metallurgical Industries (Federación Colombiana de Industrias Metalúrgicas, FEDEMETAL), the National Federation of Merchants (Federación Nacional de Comerciantes, FENALCO), and the National Association of Financial Institutions (Asociación Nacional de Instituciones Financieras, ANIF), published an analysis of Colombian problems. It did not limit itself to issues directly affecting the economic activities of its members. Rather, general issues such as inflation, lack of housing for the poor, and the minimum wage were considered and solutions proposed. In so doing, the Frente was aggregating interests as political parties are supposed to do.

The continued importance of the trade associations was apparent in 1991 when, for the first time in the history of the country and with the support of President Gaviria, they agreed to set up a special entity to negotiate with the government on issues of international trade, foreign investment, and world cooperation. The National Gremial Council was supported by thirteen organizations: ANDI, the Colombian Agriculturalists' Society (Sociedad de Agricultores de

Colombia, SAC), FENALCO, FEDEMETAL, CAMACOL, the National Association of Exporters (Asociación Nacional de Exportadores, ANALDEX), the National Federation of Livestock Raisers (Federación Nacional de Ganaderos, FEDEGAN), the Union of Colombian Insurers (Unión de Aseguradoras de Colombianos FASECOLDA), the Colombian Bankers' Association (Asociación Bancaria de Colombia, ASOBANCARIA), the Association of Sugarcane Producers and Exporters (Asociación de Productores y Exportadores de Caña de Azucar, ASOCAÑA), the Colombian Association of Plastics Industries (Asociación Colombiana de Indústrias Plásticas, ACOPLASTICOS), the Colombian Association of Small Industrialists (Asociación Colombiana de Pequeños Industriales, ACOPI), and the Colombian Association of Automobile Parts Manufacturers (Asociación Colombiana de Fabricantes de Autopartes, ACOLFA).[17] The idea of creating the council arose from a suggestion of the minister of development, Ernesto Samper Pizano.[18] The council was to make recommendations to the government and comment on any step the government might take in the direction of "economic opening." As Sabas Pretelt de la Vega, president of FENALCO, put it, "Now that we are united we hope that we will not be learning about economic policies by reading the press."[19]

Labor Unions

Organized labor in Colombia is politically weak. The first national labor federation was the Confederation of Colombian Workers (Confederación de Trabajadores Colombianos, CTC), founded in 1936 during the first administration of Alfonso López Pumarejo and with his support. With the end of the Liberal hegemony, the CTC, with its Liberal connections, was repressed by the Ospina administration. The Union of Colombian Workers (Unión de Trabajadores Colombianos, UTC), founded by the Jesuits, was allowed to flourish during the Conservative years. Both the UTC and the CTC supported the movement against Rojas Pinilla, although the former had grown rapidly under the dictatorship. Both were supporters of the National Front; however, it is safe to conclude that their power was considerably less than that of the producer associations during that period.

Two other labor federations emerged in the 1960s and 1970s. One, the Workers' Union Confederation of Colombia (Confederación Sindical de Trabajadores de Colombia CSTC), was formed in 1964 when numerous Communist–oriented unions, having been ejected from the CTC, banded together. The other, the General Confederation of Labor (Confederación General de Trabajo, CGT), a socialist and radical-Christian group, was formed in 1971. Both the CSTC and the CGT operated without legal recognition until 1974. A number of unions at the enterprise level remain unaffiliated with any of the four federations. Estimates in the mid-1980s gave the following breakdown of union membership: UTC, 19 percent; CTC, 13 percent; CSTC, 10 percent; CGT, 5 percent; other and unaffiliated, 53 percent.[20]

Several factors account for labor's weak position in Colombian politics. Labor leaders are still required to be full-time workers—a requirement that is enforced selectively. The division of labor into various federations has had obvious detrimental effects on the movement. Perhaps most important, the percentage of the labor force that is unionized is small—only 17 to 19 percent in 1974, although the percentages were higher in industry, utilities, transportation, and communication—and labor legislation has promoted the development of *enterprise* unions and weakened the possibilities for *industrywide* ones. Further, strikes in manufacturing are limited by law to forty days prior to compulsory binding arbitration. This stipulation weakens that key resource of organized labor, the ability to paralyze the economy through strikes.

The Poor

The poor, the majority of Colombians, are the least organized. To the extent that there has been organization, it has usually been directed by elite political leaders. During the National Front, governments (along with various private agencies) made efforts at "community development" aimed at increasing the material well-being of poor people (primarily campesinos but also urban dwellers) through community self-help projects such as schools and sewage systems and diminishing their passivity in the face of change. U.S. Peace Corps volunteers played an active role in this process, but local programs often collapsed when the volunteers returned home. An affiliate of the UTC (known as the National Agrarian Association) was set up to organize the rural poor, and in the mid-1970s it claimed to have 100,000 peasant members. The most ambitious effort to organize the campesinos was Lleras Restrepo's National Association of Peasants (Asociación Nacional de Usuarios Campesinos, ANUC). By the end of his presidency in August 1970, almost 1 million peasants had been recruited to the organization.[21] By August 1971, the ANUC (through its board of directors) had decided to divorce itself completely from all existing political parties and factions, judging them incapable of responding to the demands of the peasantry. Its First Peasant Mandate called for expropriation of large landholdings without indemnification and free land distribution. This radicalization and the ensuing land invasions, occupations of government buildings, boycotts, demonstrations, and other disruptive activities brought the ANUC into direct conflict with the government of Conservative President Pastrana. The response of the government was to divide, coopt, and repress. The more radical (majority) sector within the ANUC was excluded from agrarian policymaking and repressed; the moderate wing was given office space in the Ministry of Labor.

The Armed Forces

After the dissolution of Gran Colombia in 1830, most of the Venezuelan officers who had come with Bolívar had either left or been expelled from the country. The military was placed under an intellectual who reduced its size to under 2,500 men. It was controlled by the Congress, that is, the civilian elite. Throughout the rest of the nineteenth century, the military remained weak. It played only a small role in the numerous civil wars, which were largely led by amateur officer-politicians from the two political parties.[22]

The first steps toward institutionalization came in the first decade of the twentieth century, following the disastrous War of the Thousand Days and the loss of Panamá. President Rafael Reyes asked for and was granted a mission of the Chilean army, and from this mission in 1907 emerged the Escuela Militar. Yet the military remained small (proportionally the smallest in Latin America in 1932) and was slow to develop a sense of professionalism. Liberal-Conservative cleavages divided the officer corps.

The military began growing with a border dispute with Peru in 1932–1933, and the end of World War II found it stronger and more united than ever before. By 1946 the military had been out of active politics for forty years, but the Conservative governments used the military for partisan purposes during La Violencia, and in 1953 it took over power.

In the early years of the National Front, the military assumed primary responsibility for the planning and implementation of counterinsurgency to end La Violencia. This change in its role was reinforced when, in 1961, the Latin American policy of the U.S. government shifted to one of military assistance for internal security. By 1962 the Colombian military, with U.S. assistance, was involved in developing antiguerrilla operations, intelligence techniques, and military civic-action programs. At the same time, it grew from 23,000 in 1961 to 53,000 in 1966 and by 1980 had reached 64,000.

In the years since the end of the National Front, the role of the military in Colombian politics has increased. The resurgence of guerrilla activity in 1975 forced an increase in its counterinsurgency actions. Within a month of Turbay's inauguration, Minister of Defense General Luis Carlos Camacho Leyva announced an all-out offensive against the guerrillas, and with the Security Statute the military was given the power to try offenders. A vigorous campaign in 1979 led to the arrest of some 1,000 people, including artists and intellectuals, many of whom reported having been tortured. In 1980–1981 a search-and-destroy strategy was used in the El Pato–Guayabero region of Caquetá, displacing thousands of campesinos. In 1981 large numbers of troops were successful in defeating an M-19 invasion in the south.

The most recent infusion of U.S. aid to the military has been to fight drugs, including some US$65 million in equipment after the Galán assassination. The Colombian military was reluctant to be drawn into antidrug activities, considering them a police rather than an armed forces function. When it was alleged that it was using the funds to fight guerrillas rather than drug dealers, the task was given back to the national police in 1991.

On at least three occasions individual military leaders have seen fit to call attention to the basic problems of the society. In 1981 the commander of the army, General Fernando Landazábal Reyes, wrote in *Army Review,* "We are convinced that the army can militarily destroy the guerrillas, but we are also convinced that even with this, subversion will continue as long as the objective and subjective conditions in the economic, social, and political areas, which daily impair and disrupt stability, are not modified."[23] Along with the others who earlier had made similar statements, Landazábal was ultimately relieved of his post.

There was substantial military opposition to the Betancur national dialogue, and when the M-19 seized the Palacio de Justicia in 1985 some Bogotá pundits wondered if the president was really in control of the troops. The same sentiments were expressed in December 1990 when the army attacked the FARC headquarters. Yet when in August 1991 President Gaviria named a civilian minister of defense—the first since the 1940s—the Colombian military simply accepted the decision, some even arguing that it was a healthy change.

Colombian debates about the military during the Turbay years revolved around this question of control. Some argued that Camacho was more powerful than Turbay and that the military had plans that not even the civilian leaders were aware of. Human rights were being violated and people tortured and killed; hundreds were being held for long periods without bail and without counsel before being found innocent in courts-martial. Others countered that the military was doing no more and no less than what the elected civilians had instructed it to do. Camacho met almost daily with the president, but the latter was the one making policy. If individual military men used torture, however, they were operating against orders.

Conclusions are difficult in this area, especially as military officers are typically less open with inquiring social scientists than are civilian leaders. The guerrillas in Colombia are not yet as serious a threat to the status quo as the Tupamaros were in Uruguay, and the lower classes have not been mobilized as they were in Chile. For these reasons, as well as historical tradition, a "bureaucratic authoritarian" regime in Colombia seems unlikely at the moment.[24] The military did play a more active role under the Security Statute than at any time since at least 1958. In addition to being used in judicial and counterinsurgency activities, military forces have since been used in campaigns in drug-producing areas of the country. It seems certain, however, that at least some military officers feel that the social and economic inequities of the society must be corrected. The military still has not developed a corporate identity, and it lacks prestige. Major interest groups would view a military regime with caution and would actively oppose it if it envisioned a strong state at the expense of capitalism. In short, a military coup would meet with mixed reactions, and in military circles there would be considerable debate about what to do with power.

The Church

The Colombian Roman Catholic church has long been considered one of the strongest in Latin America. It was administratively strong during the colonial period; during the first years of independence it was economically strong as a large landowner and controller of the *censos* (church-held mortgages). After its loss of economic power it remained morally strong, as most Colombians continued to be believers. Yet the church hierarchy and the parish priests did favor the Conservatives, and this must have weakened it in the eyes of Liberals. This partisanship is seen in a 1949 statement of the National Bishops' Conference, in which the faithful were enjoined from voting for Liberal candidates who might "wish to implant civil marriage, divorce, and coeducation, which would open the doors to immorality and Communism."[25]

The Constitution of 1886 began "In the name of God, Supreme source of all authority," and in 1887 a concordat between the government and the Vatican defined the church's legal status. The church was described as an essential element of the social order and given a major role in various aspects of social life. Education at all levels was to conform to Catholic doctrine. The church was given the predominant role in registering births and the recording (and interring) of the dead. Marriage was placed under church control. Civil divorce did not exist; civil marriage for baptized Catholics was made contingent on a declaration of abandonment of the faith before a judge, posted publicly and communicated to the local bishop. The church was also given broad civil powers for the more than 60 percent of the land designated as "mission territories."[26] The concordat was renegotiated in 1973, but few powers were taken from the church. Civil divorce became possible, and public statements were no longer required for civil marriage. At the same time, the church's missionary role was extended, with provision being made for a "special canonical regime" for mission territories and "marginal zones" (urban slum areas).

Under the Constitution of 1991, however, divorce is possible even for marriages within the church, and the concordat is being renegotiated to reflect this change. Urbanization has weakened the church's power with the poor. Some priests began to support social and economic change. When Camilo Torres, educated both as a sociologist and as a priest, concluded that in Colombia in the mid-1960s to be a true Christian was to be a revolutionary, he was defrocked, and, having joined the ELN, was killed in a skirmish with the army. In 1968, a group of "rebel priests" dedicated their effort to changing the status quo, in the end failing.

Even at the top levels of the hierarchy there has been change. The periodic statements of the National Bishops' Conference of Colombia over time show a gradual moving away from a predominant concern with the Liberal party and socialism toward a concern for economic and social reform. In the 1950s the bishops gradually withdrew from partisan involvement and began emphasizing national unity and an end to La Violencia. During the National Front they embraced the regime and supported Liberal presidents as well as Conservative ones. Since then there has been a certain tension within the church hierarchy between the desire for unity and the need for a more equitable distribution of wealth, the conflict for it, perhaps, threatening that unity. This tension has led to a process of challenge and reevaluation within the hierarchy and a certain eclecticism in the bishops' statements.

In 1969, in *The Church Facing Change*, the bishops expressed great concern for social problems, an acceptance of sociological analysis, and an openness to change. They stressed the need for structural change in the economy and the society, openly discussing poverty, unemployment, and economic dependency in a call for general political reforms to make further change possible. The negative features of Colombian social life were discussed frankly, and, throughout, the call was for the bishops to look at social reality directly so as to prepare the clergy to deal with the country's social problems.

Signs of caution and withdrawal began to appear almost immediately. In 1971, *Justice in the World* analyzed the Colombian situation in structural terms: Poverty, unemployment, and social and political problems were directly addressed and explained as the result of unjust structures of power in the society. But when it came to action the bishops sought above all to avoid disrupting the unity of Colombian society and the violence that might follow. The church, they concluded, must stress unity over division and love over fear and hatred.

By 1976, in *Christian Identity in Actions for Justice*, the bishops had become so concerned with the possibility that activism in the struggle for social change would divide the church that the conclusions were completely different. The Catholic left and liberation theology were bitterly criticized. It was argued that eschatological principles of the traditional Catholic faith could not be transformed into purely temporal ideas. As Daniel Levine points out,

> They reject the transformation of the poor of the Gospels into the proletariat, the conversion of sin into social injustice, and the identification of evangelization with the promotion of social change and *concientización*. This transformation of religious concepts is seen as an attack on the very bases of the Catholic religion, removing its transcendental essence while undermining the recognized authority of the bishops—successors to the Apostles.[27]

Liberation theology was deemed imprudent as policy and wrong as theology. This did not mean that the bishops were abandoning the search for social reform. Rather, they were rejecting the direct leadership of the church, which more properly would stimulate others to action. These others (capable lay people) would be guided by "authentic and authoritative" expositions of Catholic doctrine—that is to say, those provided by the bishops.

In late 1981 the bishops again pointed out that Colombia's insecurity, immorality, and crime were caused by the inequalities of the social system, which they termed "an inventory of abominations." In 1991 church leaders expressed concern over the loss of life from all kinds of violence; the bishop of Pereira, for example, very vocally opposed the activities of a local clean-up squad. There is, however, no indication that the Colombian church is likely to espouse liberation theology.

The hierarchy has regularly spoken out when politicians raise the possibility of changes in areas considered to be church domain. For example, when during the presidential election of 1982 candidate López suggested the possibility of easier divorce, the bishops responded,

> No one who does not wish to commit treason to his faith can favor electoral plat-
> forms that include sharp blows to matrimony and to the family, that propose divorce
> in sacred matrimony, that aim to legalize the crime of abortion, that favor steriliza-
> tion, that support antinatalist campaigns including methods that contradict the
> teachings of the church, that recommend materialist and lay education that closes the
> doors to the messages of the faith. In the face of such proposals and the degree to
> which they may violate divine law, the Christian is obligated by conscience to abstain
> from favoring them with his vote.[28]

During the 1991 Constituent Assembly one archbishop stated, "No matter how often it is said that the Constitution approves divorce in the case of Catholic mar-riage, we affirm and will always teach, in accordance with Catholic faith and doc-trine, that valid matrimony is indissoluble and that the annulling of the civil ef-fects of sacramental marriages cannot destroy the relationship."[29]

The U.S. Government

At times in recent years the U.S. government has played an active role in Colom-bian public policy. During the Alliance for Progress years (1961–1965), the Agency for International Development (AID) mission was important in policy decisions in a number of areas; agrarian reform, education, and population control were perhaps the most important. The Military Assistance Program has had effects on the armaments, tactics, and strategy of the Colombian military, and embassy offi-cials have helped shape Colombian policy in the drug field. The Drug Enforcement Administration has played a major role since at least the early 1980s. Today there is less foreign aid than before; indeed, the López Michelsen govern-ment asked AID to leave the country. Perhaps this means a loss of influence. Yet there is too much in the historical record to discount the U.S. government as a pertinent interest group.

Group Dynamics

Government-Institution Relationships

Colombia is not a perfect corporatist society, with the economic and social groups controlled by the political elite, but neither is it a pluralistic system in which groups are formed and operate with nearly complete freedom from gov-ernment control. Some argue that although the government has the power to deny groups legal recognition, it is a power seldom exercised. We have seen that the CGT and the CSTC existed for some time before they were granted legal recognition, and the radicals in the ANUC were repressed by the Pastrana government. The safest conclusion is that legal recognition is used selectively in Colombia rather than consistently as in other Latin American systems.

Further, the interrelationships between some interest groups and the government are apparent. FEDECAFE's eleven-member national governing committee includes five ex officio members—the ministers of foreign relations, economic development, finance, and agriculture and the government-appointed manager of the Agrarian Credit Bank. The superintendent of banking (a government official) supervises its financial transactions, the president of the country appoints its manager from a list of three nominated by its national committee, and the manager acts as Colombia's official representative in international coffee negotiations. FEDECAFE's director sits on the board of directors of the Banco de la República and is a member of the CONPES. ANDI has no governmental appointees on its governing board, but it has representatives on more than a dozen governmental committees and boards of decentralized institutes at the national level and even more representatives on lower-level and industrial committees. Other groups have similar institutionalized connections with the government. Some even receive financial support from the national treasury. In short, this is not pluralism.

Family Relationships

Family relationships are extremely important in Colombian politics. It is no doubt significant that, at one point in the late 1970s, the president of the Senate and the head of ANDI were brothers. Sons or daughters following fathers in political careers have already been mentioned: Alfonso López Michelsen after Alfonso López Pumarejo, María Eugenia Rojas de Moreno Díaz after Gustavo Rojas Pinilla, Alvaro Gómez after Laureano Gómez, Andrés Pastrana after Misael Pastrana, and others.

Family relationships are extended beyond blood lines through the patronage-based *rosca* (clique). Belonging to the *rosca* of someone in office is very important. No doubt thousands of individual careers, not only in the ministries but also elsewhere in the non-civil service bureaucracy, depend on who wins the presidential election every four years.

As Francisco Leal Buitrago and Andrés Dávila Ladrón de Guevara have recently described it, while giving social mobility to some individuals the system is resistant to change. They are critical of the indiscriminate use of governmental financial resources for political bargaining and the tendency for the manipulation of governmental resources to become the major task of political leaders.[30]

Informal Ties

Informal ties are no doubt more important than formal ones. Members of the Colombian elite have much in common. They not only have the same social background but also have gone to the same universities and may belong to the same exclusive clubs. Under the circumstances, it is reasonable to ask if simply changing a constitution is sufficient to change behavior.

Notes

1. *El Espectador* (Bogotá), May 28, 1990.

2. *El Espectador* (Bogotá), July 29, 1990, my translation.

3. Confidential interview with a former minister of mines and petroleum, May 28, 1981.

4. Confidential interview with a former minister of economic development, April 10, 1981.

5. Confidential interview with a former minister of the treasury, April 20, 1981.

6. Miguel Urrutia, "Diversidad ideológica e integración Andiana," *Coyuntura Económica* 10 (1980):197.

7. Confidential interview with a former minister of the treasury, April 20, 1981.

8. The information for this section comes from Angel Israel Rivera Ortiz, "The Politics of Development Planning in Colombia" (Ph.D diss., State University of New York at Buffalo, 1976), 65, 67, 71, 76, 77, 104.

9. *Latin America Weekly Report,* November 13, 1981.

10. Fals Borda, *Subversión y cambio social,* 117.

11. Statement at the Universidad de los Andes, Bogotá, 1981.

12. Luis Carlos Galán, "El nuevo liberalismo," *El Tiempo* (Bogotá), June 8, 1981.

13. Gary Hoskin, "The Colombian Party System: Electoral Domination and System Instability," paper presented at the U.S. State Department Conference on Colombia, Washington, D.C., November 9, 1981, 31.

14. Confidential interview with a Colombian sociologist, Bogotá, May 29, 1994.

15. The information for this section comes from Hartlyn, "Interest Groups and Political Conflict."

16. This point was brought to my attention by Jonathan Hartlyn.

17. *El Tiempo* (Bogotá), July 24, 1991.

18. *El Espectador* (Bogotá), July 24, 1991.

19. *El Tiempo* (Bogotá), March 31, 1986, my translation.

20. Information for this section comes from Bagley, "Political Power, Public Policy, and the State" and "Beyond the National Front: State and Society in Contemporary Colombia," paper presented at the U.S. State Department Conference on Colombia, Washington, D.C., November 9, 1981.

21. Information in this section and the following one comes from Premo, "The Armed Forces and Colombian Politics."

22. Ruhl, *Colombia,* 18.

23. Quoted in Premo, "The Armed Forces and Colombian Politics," 31.

24. J. Mark Ruhl, "An Alternative to the Bureaucratic-Authoritarian Regime: The Case of Colombian Modernization," *Inter-American Economic Affairs* 35 (1981), suggests that the lack of populist parties in Colombia is one of the major reasons that there has been no bureaucratic authoritarianism.

25. Martz, *Colombia,* 84.

26. This analysis is based on Daniel H. Levine, *Religion and Politics in Latin America: The Catholic Church in Venezuela and Colombia* (Princeton: Princeton University Press, 1981), esp. 70–96.

27. Ibid., 92–93.

28. *El Espectador* (Bogotá), March 14, 1982, my translation.

29. *El Tiempo* (Bogotá), July 4, 1991, my translation.

30. Francisco Leal Buitrago and Andrés Dávila Ladrón de Guevera, *Clientelismo: El sistema político y su expresión regional* (Bogotá: Tercer Mundo Editores), 354.

6

THE COLOMBIAN MIXED ECONOMY AND PUBLIC POLICY

MANY COLOMBIANS ASSUME THAT ECONOMIC conditions are a cause of the country's problems. Although surely not marxist, they argue that poor people become guerrillas or engage in organized drug-related activities because of the lack of opportunities in the legal economy. Guerrilla truces do not work, they continue, because, failing to find work, the amnestied turn to ordinary crime. The drug trade has given income to thousands of Colombians who have neither the education nor the personal connections to get employment in the legal economy. Hence any solution to the problems of the country must begin with a resolution of the poverty of the country and the maldistribution of income.

The Colombian Economy Today

When one thinks of the Colombian economy, coffee usually first comes to mind. This is a correct first impression in one sense but a misleading one in another. Coffee has usually been the leading legal export (although it has been superseded by crude petroleum in recent years), and investment in capital goods, which are usually imported, has historically been highly dependent on coffee earnings. However, coffee production makes up only about 4 percent of the gross domestic product (GDP), and increase in GDP is not highly dependent on coffee earnings, at least in the short run.[1]

The economy today is still predominantly a primary-sector one. This sector (agriculture, fishing, and mining) makes up 25 percent of GDP (down from 39 percent in 1950–1951). The manufacturing sector is 22 percent of GDP (up from 17 percent in 1950–1951). Other economic activities include commerce (12 percent), government services (8 percent), construction and electricity (5 percent), and transportation (9 percent). An "other activities" category makes up the final 20 percent.[2] Many of these changes are the result of explicit governmental policy.

A recent development is the importance of the "other economy" based on illegal trade. Although contraband is an old Colombian tradition in border regions, the 1970s witnessed an order-of-magnitude increase, primarily through the growth of the illicit drug trade. It is clear that the drug trade has had a positive effect on Colombia's economy, but the exact amount of money entering the country is unclear. One recent figure from the Colombian government is that US$10 billion entered the country from the drug trade in the 1980s.

Colombia's economic performance since World War II has been satisfactory but not spectacular. Annual growth of GDP averaged 5.1 percent during the 1960s (below the average of 6.1 percent for "middle-income" developing countries) and 6.0 percent from 1970 to 1979 (above the 5.5 percent average for those countries). At no time were slowdowns long-lasting; most of them lasted less than a year. Then in 1979 the growth rate declined to 5.1 percent and in 1980 to between 3 and 4 percent.[3] The 1980s were not good years in Colombia, though not as bad as in the rest of Latin America. An Inter-American Development Bank Report near the end of the decade stated that Colombia had experienced the highest per capita GDP growth rate in the area and one of the lowest inflation rates.[4] These were years of export diversification (see Table 6.1). By 1989 the leading exports were coffee (23 percent), petroleum (23 percent), coal (10 percent), textiles (7 percent), and "others" (37 percent). The monoculture typical of Colombia had obviously been left behind.

Trade with the United States, although a great deal less important than thirty years ago, still accounted for 37 percent of all exports and 35 percent of all imports in 1988. Coffee's proportion of legal export earnings fell until the coffee "boom" of the late 1970s and again until a smaller "boom" in the mid-1980s; the percentage of coffee going to the United States has fallen to about 21 percent (1983–1987), with West Germany occupying the first position (30 percent). Imports are machinery and transport equipment (29 percent in 1988), chemicals (20 percent), metals (12 percent), and "others" (29 percent), primarily consumer goods.[5] In short, while Colombia is still a country that exports primary goods and imports manufactured ones, it is no longer a country that trades predominantly in one product with one advanced industrial country.

In the period between 1967 and 1990, in particular, the economy did not fit neatly into a category of "capitalist," "socialist," or even "state capitalist." The state was considered to have a primary role in leading the nation out of underdevelop-

TABLE 6.1   Colombian Foreign Trade, 1970–1990

Year	Exports (US$ Millions)	Percent Coffee	Imports (US$ Millions)
1970	643	59	598
1971	656	52	652
1972	841	49	702
1973	1,009	48	1,117
1974	1,214	41	1,117
1975	1,414	44	1,403
1976	1,652	51	1,312
1977	2,243	61	1,843
1978	2,569	66	2,188
1979	3,410	59	3,031
1980	3,945	60	4,663
1981	2,956	48	5,199
1982	3,095	50	5,478
1983	3,081	30	4,968
1984	3,483	39	4,492
1985	3,552	49	4,131
1986	5,108	52	3,852
1987	5,024	40	4,228
1988	5,026	32	5,005
1989	6,324	23	6,716
1990	7,152	20	5,589

SOURCES: 1970–1978: "Análisis del sector externo colombiano," *Revista ANDI* 48 (1980): 54–55; 1979, División de Estudios Económicos, DANE, "El comercio exterior colombiano en 1979," *Revista Mensual de Estadística* 348 (1980):34. Exports and Imports, 1980–1990: *Colombia Today* 25, 3 (1990). Coffee percentage: 1980–1982, 1985, *Anuario de Comercio Exterior*; 1983, *Economic Review of Colombia, Ecuador* (London), November 20, 1984; 1984, *Colombia Today* 19, 11 (1984); 20, 11 (1985); 1985, 1986, Ibid., 22, 9 (1987); 1987, Ibid., 23, 10 (1988/89); 1988, Ibid., 24, 9 (1989/90); 1989–1990; Ibid., 26, 4 (1992).

ment. It owned most infrastructure (roads, railroads, and telecommunications) and other costly but important activities (electricity). It was expected that it would develop energy resources, since with few exceptions subsoil rights were its patrimony. It also was expected to undertake any project considered essential for national development when private investment declined to do so, typically selling such an enterprise once it was established (as with the Paz del Rio steel mill).

This tradition, going back to the Spanish colony, had been even stronger in the nineteenth century, but the growth of private capital—especially in the Medellín area—eventually made the state's role in the economy among the weakest in Latin America. It was generally assumed that the private sector could operate more efficiently, and there was little indication of a "state ideology" at the higher levels of the state itself. Yet the state's involvement through taxation, tariff and exchange rates, and policy toward other countries and multinational corporations remained extremely important.

Historical Development

The Colombian economy has been a dependent one, responding more to economic conditions outside the country than to those inside it. The relevant external factors have been the developed economies of the world—particularly European countries in the nineteenth century, the United States between 1900 and 1969, and the United States, Japan, and the European Economic Community countries since 1970. The growth of the Colombian economy can be classified into five periods: 1830–1880, classic dependency with no stable export crop; 1880–1930, classic dependency with a stable export crop; 1930–1967, dependent development with emphasis on import substitution; 1967–1988, dependent development with emphasis on export diversification; and 1988 to the present, neoliberalism.

1830–1880

The period of classic dependency, characterized by the exchange of primary products for foreign manufactured goods, was an unstable one because Colombia had no stable export product. Fluctuations in the quantity and value of exports of gold, quinine, tobacco, and other products gave the country hard currencies with which to buy manufactured goods, primarily from Britain. Colombian leaders saw this as a desirable path for the country even if it did do harm to some native artisan industry. The period was one of nineteenth-century economic liberalism, and within Colombia the Liberal party was in power for most of the time. An explicit statement of this division of labor was made in 1948 by Treasury Secretary Florentino González:

> In a country rich in mines and agricultural products, which can sustain a considerable and beneficial export trade, the latter should not attempt to encourage industries that distract the inhabitants from the agricultural and mining occupations. . . . Europe with an intelligent population, and with the possession of steam power and its applications, educated in the art of manufacturing, is fulfilling its mission in the industrial world by giving various forms to raw materials. We too should fulfill our mission, and there is no doubt as to what it is, if we consider the profusion of natural resources with which Providence has endowed this land. We should offer Europe raw materials and open our doors to her manufactures, to facilitate trade and the profit it brings, and to provide the consumer, at a reasonable price, with the products of the manufacturing industry.[6]

1880–1930

The second period was different from the first in that coffee represented a stable export crop; earnings from coffee exports could be used for manufactured imports. By 1878 coffee earnings represented 13.5 percent of total exports, and the percentages increased rapidly after that, reaching a high of 80 percent in 1924.[7] With this situation came increasing dependence on the United States. Whereas earlier products had been traded with a variety of nations, coffee went predominantly to the Colossus of the north, particularly after World War I. Imports were less concentrated than exports, but here again the majority came from the United States. Import-substitution industrialization began as early as the first decade of this century and increased during the trade cutoff of World War I. It was, however, the years of the Great Depression that saw a quantum leap in this industrialization. Foreign trade became more important than ever, as industrialization had been achieved with imported capital goods.

1930–1967

In the third period, coffee exports were encouraged in order to buy capital goods. Other products were exported, some through multinational enclaves (bananas, petroleum, which became the second-largest "traditional" export, and gold, with foreign companies increasingly purchasing Colombian mines), but in 1964, for example, coffee made up 79 percent of export earnings. The problem with a single dominant export was obvious: World coffee prices fluctuated according to supply and demand. When frost in Brazil led to temporary shortages and hence higher prices, Colombian export earnings boomed. When world supply normalized—and when the new nations of Africa entered the market—prices plummeted, and so did the ability to import.

Perhaps all Colombian politicians since the National Front have agreed on the need for "economic development," but there have been recurrent debates about what economic development is and how to achieve it. The debate on defining development has centered on whether it is more than economic growth. In the early 1980s *Estrategia Económica y Financiera,* a leading Bogotá economic journal, stated that Colombia could be a developed country in twenty years. Asked just what was meant by this, one of the editors replied, "We mean that Colombia will have a gross domestic product per capita equal to that of Spain—or even Italy—today."[8] Other Colombians argue that the economic development comes only with diversification of the economy and/or less dependency on foreign capital, technology, and know-how. Some of these people also consider redistribution of wealth to be at least as important as mere economic growth.

The people in power have usually defined development as growth and proceeded to debate the best way to achieve it. Should coffee be emphasized as Colombia's natural "comparative advantage," or should growth come through import substitution and/or more diversified exports? What is the appropriate role of the manufacturing sector? Should a high rate of exchange be maintained to encourage exports or a low rate to encourage imports? How important is the control of inflation? In making economic policy the president plays the key role. If he is unwilling or unable to achieve coordination—through threats, promises, and persuasion—there will surely be none. At the same time, the vested interests of the trade associations, Colombian and multinational, may prevent the most able president from implementing public policy.

The first two National Front presidents had as their main priority the reestablishment of peace in the countryside. This policy was largely successful. The same could not be said about other public policies. The presidency of Alberto Lleras Camargo saw the enactment of Law 135, which was designed to:

- eliminate and prevent the inequitable concentration of land and/or its subdivision into uneconomic units; reconstitute adequate units of cultivation in the *minifundio* zones; provide lands to those who lacked them;

- promote adequate economic use of unused and deficiently used lands, by means of programs designed to secure their well-balanced distribution and rational utilization;

- increase farm productivity by the application of appropriate techniques; endeavor to have land used in the way best-suited to its location and characteristics;

- give small tenants and sharecroppers greater guarantees of security of tenure and make it easier for them and for wage laborers to gain ownership of land;

- elevate the level of living of the rural population through the measures already indicated and through the coordination and promotion of services for technical assistance, agricultural credit, housing, marketing, health and social security, storage and preservation of products, and the promotion of services for technical assistance, agricultural credit, housing, marketing, health and social security, storage and preservation of products, and the promotion of cooperatives;

- insure the conservation, defense, improvement, and adequate utilization of natural resources.

To implement Law 135, a Colombian Agrarian Reform Institute (*Instituto Colombiano de la Reforma Agraria*, INCORA) was created, staffed originally with young lawyers, economists, and sociologists who were seriously interested in changing the structure of land tenure.[9] The program was eventually supported (and in part financed) by the Alliance for Progress.

This agrarian reform proved largely a failure. The original proposal, drafted by Carlos Lleras Restrepo, had gone much farther, but it was watered down during congressional consideration and then never effectively implemented. Although land titles were given to 54,000 families between 1961 and 1967, some 400,000 to 500,000 families were landless. The total land distributed was 4,275,000 hectares (10,556,000 acres); of this, 46 percent came from colonization of public lands and only about 1 percent from expropriations.[10]

The Conservative Guillermo León Valencia (1962–1966) continued many of Lleras Camargo's policies, although he lacked the inclination or ability to coordinate the disparate governmental and economic interests. His administration is remembered as an ineffectual one.

1967–1988

The Lleras Restrepo Administration. By the time of the inauguration of Carlos Lleras Restrepo (1966), the economy had suffered from almost a decade of low coffee prices and the resultant trade deficits, it was apparent that the Lleras Camargo land reform had failed, and there had been little public policymaking for at least four years. The new president was a trained economist with definite ideas about how things should be changed and the ability to coordinate the government. Policy changes during his presidency came through four initiatives: Decree-Law 444, another agrarian reform, the first Colombian population policy, and the creation of the Andean Pact.

Enacted in 1967, Decree-Law 444 marked the beginning of the fourth period of Colombian economic history, that of dependent development with emphasis on export diversification. Diversified exports, rather than either coffee exports or import-substitution industrialization (which had reached limits in Colombia later to be seen in other Latin American countries because of the lack of the growth of intermediary goods and capital-goods sectors), were to become the "motor" for development. The law decreed a simple and general tax credit for the export of "minor" products (that is, all except coffee and petroleum). A general tax-credit certificate (*certificado de abono tributario,* CAT), originally set at 15 percent of the export value, was given to minor exporters and could be used in payment of taxes one year after the date of issue. The CATs were freely negotiable. Law 444 also set up an Export Promotion Fund (Fondo de Promoción de Exportaciones, PROEXPO), a decentralized institute that channeled credit under liberal terms to exporters, provided equity capital under special circumstances, insured against political and noncommercial export risks, helped prepare export plans, attempted to promote an "export mentality" in Colombia, and advertised and held trade fairs abroad.[11]

Although minor exports had been encouraged by earlier laws, Decree-Law 444 had a much greater effect. These exports grew rapidly (15 percent in the first two years alone) and by 1974 had become more important than coffee (petroleum was no longer being exported). These minor exports (especially bananas, cotton, sugar, and tobacco but also gold, paper and cardboard, meat, wood, shoes, seafood, glass, oilseed cakes, chemicals, furs, cement, hides, precious stones, tires, books, fresh-cut flowers, and dog toys[12]) provided foreign exchange to purchase consumer, capital, and intermediate goods. Although dependency had not been left behind, the monoculture seemed to have been abandoned. The adoption of Decree-Law 444 did not, however, mean that coffee was neglected. Every Colombian government since 1967 has been supportive of coffee production and exportation, and a close relationship exists between governments and FEDECAFE. Minor exports were to supplement coffee exports rather than replace them, and until the late 1980s import-substitution industrialization was not discouraged but was simply no longer a major goal.

A second part of Decree-Law 444 regulated foreign companies for the first time. Article I stated that foreign private investment had to be in harmony with the national interest. Any private investment greater than US$100,000 required government approval. A complex institutional machinery was set up to enforce the stipulations. The DNP analyzed and approved investment proposals; the Exchange Office registered and authorized the outflow of capital; the superintendent of foreign trade (the director of INCOMEX) granted import licenses; the Advisory Committee on Global Licenses was in charge of implementing government policies on capital-goods imports and avoiding excess unused productive capacity.[13] The Lleras government's intention was to gather accurate data on foreign investment, to control repatriation of profits (a limit of 14 percent of investment was set), and to make certain that foreign competition did not force Colombian enterprises out of business.

Decree-Law 444 was a response to a very real problem. Foreign investment in Colombia, especially that from the United States after World War I, had sizable interests in high-technology and service fields. By the end of 1966 total foreign investment was US$466 million, particularly in the fields of chemicals, pharmaceuticals, food, tires, and electrical machinery,[14] and some Colombians considered it significant enough to be controlled.

A third element of Decree-Law 444 was the establishment of a "crawling-peg" exchange rate. Previously, a set exchange rate had led to balance-of-payments crises and to large devaluations. After Decree-Law 444 there were continuing small devaluations, arising to a degree from "free-market" transactions but with the government still playing a role. In theory, these devaluations were to keep up with inflation and by and large this was true in practice until the mid-1970s, when for political reasons the peso was allowed to be overvalued.

With Law 1 of 1968, an attempt was made to accelerate the pace of land distribution by eliminating the legal and financial restrictions that had slowed or prevented the application of provisions of Law 135 of 1961. The new law was also intended to increase production in the commercial agricultural sector by reorganizing state credit mechanisms, increasing the total amount of resources available for agriculture, and providing tax incentives for exporting nontraditional agricultural products (that is, other than coffee and cattle).[15] This law had a redistributive orientation and some redistributive effects. INCORA's activities increased, with over half of all negotiated purchases and almost two-thirds of all expropriations of the period 1961–1971 taking place in the last two years of the period. Nevertheless, by the end of the Lleras presidency the impact of the agrarian reform program on the country's land tenure system was still extremely limited.

Despite the fact that the 1964 census showed that the Colombian population had grown by 3 percent annually since 1951, the Lleras Restrepo administration was to advocate smaller families and slower population growth. (Alberto Lleras, who had done so as a private citizen in 1965, had been criticized by the church hierarchy.)[16] Lleras Restrepo was the only Latin American president to sign the Declaration on Population of the United Nations (UN). In the same year (1966) the Ministry of Health signed a contract for a program of training and research that included family planning in addition to maternal and child health. In 1967 about 35,000 women received family-planning services in one of the private clinics supported by foreign donors (AID, the Rockefeller and Ford Foundations, and international agencies based in Sweden and Canada). That number had grown to 164,000 by 1972, and a survey conducted in mid-1973 in Bogotá indicated that about half of the women were using some form of artificial contraception. By 1991, when the population of the country was estimated as nearly 32 million, the growth rate had declined to 1.7 percent a year. A survey indicated that 66 percent of women, either married or living in common-law arrangements, used artificial birth control.[17] In 1990, 88 percent of pregnant women received prenatal care, while 85 percent had medical services during delivery. (The percentages were lower in rural areas, 71 and 60 percent respectively.)[18]

Much of the impetus for this population policy came from foreign sources, which between 1965 and 1972 donated a total close to US$15 million for the purpose. The church was the only organized group that opposed it; medical personnel recognized the human cost of rapid population growth, and planners understood the economic costs.[19] The result was the most thorough antinatalist policy in any Latin American country. Although population growth was declining even before the Lleras policy, few would argue that family-planning clinics had no effect on the change.

The Pastrana Administration. The Pastrana government (1970–1974) continued many of the Lleras Restrepo policies, but in agrarian reform and construction there were notable changes. The Pastrana economic policy centered on the leading-sector concept—emphasis on one sector with multiplier effects on the rest of the economy. The sector chosen was construction, particularly in the cities. It was argued that many unskilled people could be put to work in that sector, and when they spent their earnings the multiplier effect would benefit much of the rest of the country. This strategy had the advantage that it could be carried out with few imports.

To encourage private investment, the government established a constant-value investment in which deposits increased not only with interest but also with an inflation factor (*unidades de poder adquisitivo constante*, UPAC). Mortgages were also corrected for inflation, and soon many other things were "UPACed": life insurance benefits (and premiums) and, much less formally, wages and prices. The UPAC concept and the overheating of the economy with massive investment in construction led to general inflation, which reached a high of 27 percent in 1974.

These years also produced one last attempt at agrarian reform. After his narrow victory over Rojas Pinilla, Pastrana promised redistributive reforms in a number of areas. The land-reform proposal, however, contained several aspects that were very threatening to the large agricultural groups. Most important was the tax on the estimated income of agricultural land, based on a complex formula taking into account such factors as region, type of crop or livestock, soil quality, and climatic conditions.[20] This controversial idea led to bargaining among the different factions of the political parties and the different agricultural groups that ended in major concessions to the large landowners with regard to land taxes and large infusions of new credit into the sector for capital-intensive agricultural development. It is not surprising that little land redistribution followed. Indeed, one expert has termed these laws as "the counterreform," meaning quite simply that agricultural production had become more important than redistribution of land.[21] Organized groups were able to block and water down laws; enforcement was difficult because of the lack of trained personnel and because landowners could tie up the reform in lengthy litigation. Further, after the mid-1960s when it had become evident that there would be no other Castros in Latin America, even AID officials stressed increased production instead of redistribution.

The López Michelsen Administration. When Alfonso López Michelsen was inaugurated as president on August 7, 1974, there was a certain amount of optimism. The National Front had ended, and López had been voted in by a large majority. Further, he was widely considered progressive: He had, after all, once been the leader of the MRL. In his public pronouncement and in his four-year plan, called "Closing the Gap," López called for a much more direct attack on poverty and inequality and more attention to efficiency and the control of inflation. The central theme of the plan was "to reduce the gap between country and city, the gap between rich and poor barrios, the gap between those who have access to health services and education and the illiterate and undernourished."[22]

The López government soon declared an "economic emergency," which gave it the ability to rule by decree. The economic team had been working in secret since late May, making plans for the first months, and this allowed the government to make many economic changes in a ninety-day period. Its tax reform plan covered the sales tax, export taxes and incentives, adjustments of tariffs on imports, tax treatment of government agencies, and personal and company income taxes. In general, the goals of the reform were to (1) increase the progressivity of the tax system, (2) reduce distortions in the allocation of resources, (3) promote economic stability by increasing revenue and by enhancing the built-in response of the system to growth in national income, and (4) simplify the administration of the system and thus reduce evasion and increase yields.[23]

In 1975 the new status of Colombia as a petroleum importer (at a time when the Organization of Petroleum Exporting Countries [OPEC] had increased international prices threefold), the massive influx of foreign currencies from the drug trade, and the coffee "bonanza" following the July 1974 frost in Brazil subjected the economy to intense inflationary pressure and made monetary control the key concern of economic policy. Government investments "to close the gap" had to be delayed or canceled.

Petroleum development had begun in Colombia in 1921 with the entrance of the first U.S. petroleum company (Tropical, a subsidiary of Standard of New Jersey). Gulf and other foreign companies had followed. The typical contract was a "concession" whereby the foreign company had complete control of the operation, both production and refining, and for which the government received certain taxes and royalties. By 1950, 412 million barrels of Colombian crude had been exported by foreign companies, especially to the United States.[24] In the 1960s the government was receiving only about US$0.25 per barrel.

In 1951 the first Tropical contract ended, and the area that Tropical had exploited for thirty years (the so-called Concesión de Mares) reverted to the Colombian government, as did the refinery at Barrancabermeja, the largest in the country. To continue exploitation of the area after Colombian capitalists had been offered the opportunity and refused it, the government of Laureano Gómez founded the Colombian Petroleum Enterprise (Empresa Colombiana de Petróleos, ECOPETROL). ECOPETROL soon discovered that the most accessible petroleum had already been taken and that it lacked the expertise to run the refinery. It therefore contracted with Tropical to do this for an additional ten years, during which Colombian technicians could be trained.[25]

During the Rojas Pinilla years, Cities Services offered an alternative contract to the concession model. This was the "association" contract, a kind of joint venture whereby the foreign company explored at its own risk and cost and, if an economically attractive amount of petroleum was found, invested equally with the government in production, with the government receiving royalties, taxes, and 50 percent of the petroleum. Production was managed by the multinational (as "operator"), and the entire enterprise was governed by an executive committee composed of one representative of the multinational and one of ECOPETROL, which made all major decisions by consensus.

By the time that López Michelsen was inaugurated, there had been over a decade of debate about petroleum production. It was clear that Colombian consumption was increasing (it had reached 48.5 million barrels in 1973), whereas production was stable until 1970 and declining thereafter. Therefore exports (including those of ECOPETROL after 1971) were down to fewer than 10 million barrels a year. (A total of over 1 billion barrels of crude had been exported by that time, with the highest point coming in 1965, when 40 million barrels were exported.)[26] During this extended debate, one side (the multinationals and the Colombians who agreed with them) argued that the foreign companies were doing their best and could do even better if incentives for exploration were increased. The other side (including one minister of mines who, in effect, was forced out of office by the multinationals) argued that the operators had found ample crude and were limiting production until the government gave them better prices. In any case, the country's second-largest export had become an import, and the López government responded by decreeing that all future petroleum contracts would be association ones (not, however, ending the existing concessions) and all "new" crude and crude obtained by "enhanced" recovery methods would be bought at OPEC prices, CIF Cartagena. Exploration in the following years did increase, and by the early 1980s production increased for the first time in a decade. Some politicians were content with this, arguing that the association contract was more nationalistic than the concession. Others suggested that the government was never an equal partner in such contracts, instead playing the role of "horse" to the multinational's "jockey."[27]

A related question during the López years was that of coal development. By 1974 annual coal production was in the neighborhood of 3.5 million metric tonnes (3.86 million short tons), and almost all of it was in the hands of Colombians; the great majority of production was in mining *minifundios*. The most promising Colombian coal deposit was El Cerrejón, on La Guajira peninsula. In the 1950s the Industrial Promotion Institute (Instituto de Fomento Industrial, IFI) began a series of studies of the area, and in 1969, it established a commercial enterprise, Cerrejón Carboneras, to arrange for its exploitation. In 1972 a memorandum of agreement was signed with Peabody Coal, a subsidiary of Kennecott Copper, for the Central Cerrejón area.[28]

In June 1974, the International Colombia Resources Corporation (INTERCOR), a Canadian subsidiary of Exxon, produced a draft contract for the North and South Cerrejón areas. INTERCOR proposed an association contract much like those employed in petroleum, but this contract was never signed. In October 1975 both the IFI and ECOPETROL asked the Ministry of Mines for the right to develop the northern and southern areas. ECOPETROL received that right and in the same month sent a model contract out to bid to seventeen foreign companies. The model contract was one of association. In February 1976 proposals were received from six multinationals. In the same month, the minister of mines announced that an impasse had been reached with Peabody for the central zone and Peabody was withdrawing from the country. In November 1976 the Colombian Coal Company (Carbones de Colombia, CARBOCOL) was established as a "second-level" state enterprise—one in which all the stock was owned by other state enterprises, including the IFI and ECOPETROL. In December 1976 CARBOCOL signed a contract with INTERCOR (now a U.S. subsidiary of Exxon), which offered the highest royalties (15 percent), for the North Cerrejón area. In June 1977 CARBOCOL began working in the central area in "a direct and independent" way.[29]

Alongside these developments in petroleum and coal, the drug trade began to have serious economic effects during the López years. The Colombian government has never been able to control the funds coming from illicit drugs, and no one really knows the total income from this source. Many dollars are simply not brought into the country but placed in banks and investments in other countries, although at times they have been tacitly welcomed by Colombian leaders. Drug money has been used to construct fabulous dwellings, and the earnings of the many Colombians employed in this effort and in the trade itself have had multiplier effects on the rest of the economy.

Finally, new foreign earnings from the high price of coffee as a result of frost in Brazil threatened to fuel inflation in Colombia, and the López government responded by lowering tariff barriers while making it more difficult to change dollars into Colombian pesos. Whereas the average coffee price in 1974 was US$0.78 a pound, Colombian coffee sold for an average of US$0.81 in 1975, US$1.58 in 1976, and US$2.40 in 1977. Although this increased foreign income would normally have been welcomed and quickly increased Colombia's foreign reserves, it increased the money supply too rapidly. Because the productive capacity of the economy was not similarly raised, inflation threatened to exceed the 20–30 percent a year that had been common since the Pastrana presidency. To withdraw some of the dollars from the economy, the government relaxed import restrictions, increased coffee taxes, established a waiting period for changing dollars at the full official rate, and postponed or canceled government expenditures. In an irony of a dependent economy, López Michelsen found it impossible to "close the gap," not because of the lack of foreign exchange that had so characterized governments in the 1960s but because of an excess of foreign exchange.

The Turbay Administration. In August 1978 Julio César Turbay Ayala inherited López's problems. As has every recent president, he came up with a four-year plan, in his case called the "Plan of National Integration." The goals of the plan were economic decentralization and regional autonomy, development of transportation and means of communication, development of the energy and mining sectors, and development of a new social strategy. An unstated goal was the control of inflation, which remained at 25–30 percent throughout Turbay's term.

Economic decentralization and regional autonomy proved elusive. Although the DNP was supposed to give priority to investments outside of the four major cities, most major decisions were still made in Bogotá. Investments in transportation and communication—as well as other projects—were carried out, but some were delayed because of the fear of fueling more inflation. In addition, there were new problems. By June 1981 the international coffee price was down to US$1.27 a pound; a year later it had recovered to about US$1.40. In the same time period, earnings from the drug trade were also down because of a coordinated program between the U.S. and Colombian governments and because of competition from other South American countries in cocaine and from the United States in marijuana.[30] The final year and a half of the Turbay administration were therefore characterized by declining balances of trade. Colombian international reserves increased slightly, reaching US$5.633 billion at the end of 1981.

In the energy sector, the López programs were continued. All new petroleum agreements were in association contracts; by 1978 these agreements covered almost one-quarter of the petroleum. In 1980 petroleum production increased dramatically for the first time in more than a decade; US$471 million in petroleum imports were needed in the same year, making Colombia a minor importer compared with other Third World countries.

In September 1980 Turbay and the CONPES accepted INTERCOR's "commercial declaration" for the North Cerrejón region. This declaration called for investments of nearly US$3 billion to construct a strip mine, facilities, railroad, and port that would export a minimum of 15 million metric tonnes (16.5 million short tons) of coal a year beginning in 1986.[31]

A key goal of both the López and Turbay governments was to develop another source of foreign exchange. During the López years this had hardly seemed necessary, although one of López's ministers advocated it as a way of avoiding a recurrence of the "populism" of the late 1960s and concurrent balance-of-payment difficulties and unemployment).[32] By 1980, however, people in Bogotá and Washington were talking about difficult times for the Colombian economy until the North Cerrejón mines were in full production. If one accepted Exxon's own figures, the Colombian government would earn, in taxes and royalties and from its own half of the coal, between US$48.852 billion (in current dollars, assuming production of the projected 15 million metric tonnes a year and low prices for coal) and US$100.7 billion (in current dollars, assuming production of 25 million metric tonnes [27.6 million short tons] a year and high prices).[33] The oil glut of the early 1980s led to lower coal prices than projected, and the North El Cerrejón mine operated at a loss in its first years.

The Betancur Administration. Belisario Betancur started his presidency with the hope of ameliorating conditions for the lower classes of Colombia, but the economic difficulties of the period made this largely impossible. Betancur was a populist who had the misfortune of governing during a world recession. As prices for Colombian exports stagnated, the country's economy went from bad to worse. Foreign lending agencies stopped new loans to many Latin American countries because of their excessive debt burdens, and it became harder for Colombia to obtain loans even though its debt was under control. Under the circumstances, the Betancur government turned to monitoring the International Monetary Fund, and although it was not required to do so because it was not seeking standby loans, began following the IMF guidelines—lowering its budget, setting prices at the international level, and gradually devaluing its overvalued peso. During the Betancur years devaluation exceeded inflation—especially in 1985, when the former was over 50 percent. All of this made it impossible for the populist president to do much for the poor of Colombia, and the rehabilitation of the guerrilla-affected areas was not well funded. One can only speculate what might have happened if Betancur's watch had fallen in better economic times.

1988 to the Present

The Barco Administration. During the Barco administration the economy flourished. Colombia had one of the highest growths of gross national product in Latin America, and one of the lowest inflation rates. Whereas international banks were hesitant to give new loans to other Latin American countries, the Colombian government regularly received them. A good part of the country's economic health was associated with the devaluation begun during the Betancur years. As a result, the economy depended less on one product (coffee) and more on petroleum and other minor exports. By the end of this period, however, the International Coffee Agreement of 1962 had expired, and this meant not only lower prices for Colombian coffee but also less stable prices. As the average price fell from US$1.40 to US$0.90 a pound, the country received US$200 million less in coffee revenues in 1990 than in the previous year despite selling more of its high-quality product than ever before. In 1983 Occidental Petroleum discovered the Caño Limón deposit in the Cravo Norte zone of Arauca, with reserves of 750 million barrels. Since known reserves were down to 549 million barrels in 1980, this find more than doubled them. ECOPETROL entered into association contracts in those areas, and by 1988 production was up to 429,000 barrels per day (from 197,000 in 1985) and crude petroleum was once again the second-most-important export.[34] Colombia was once again an exporting country and was even asked (but declined) to join OPEC.

Following the neoliberal philosophy, the Barco government began gradually reducing tariffs on imports. The idea was that Colombian industry had become inefficient because of its protection; the gradual reduction of tariffs would encourage the more efficient industries to modernize so as to be competitive, while those that were unable to modernize would go out of business as consumers bought cheaper imported goods.

The Gaviria Administration. César Gaviria Trujillo continued several Barco policies, indeed accelerating the economic opening. In July 1991 the government confirmed the discovery of a large petroleum field in Cusiana, in the department of Casanare, that might be larger than Caño Limón. Although final studies had not been completed, some experts estimated the reserves as 1 billion barrels. The studies were to be continued in the association contract between ECOPETROL and Triton Energy (United States), Total Compagnie (France), and British Petroleum. Given the size of the discovery, under a new sliding scale ECOPETROL was to receive 60 percent of the profits.[35]

By mid-1991 it was obvious that the change to a neoliberal model would not be an easy one. When the government decreed in late June that peso exchanges would no longer be controlled by the government but could be made in any bank, the immediate effect was a revaluation of the peso from slightly over 600 to the U.S. dollar to slightly over 500. A mechanism was established to delay the conversion of foreign earnings to pesos through a system of exchange certificates with a

A cotton plantation in Tolima (Photo courtesy of the Colombian Information Service.)

maturity of ninety days and a discount of up to 10 percent.³⁶ This situation had obvious effects on Colombian exporters, who protested that the revaluation of the peso called into question the government's commitment to opening up the economy. The president of ANDI, Carlos Angel Arango, added,

> Everything seems to indicate that the use of the exchange rate will be abandoned, leaving devaluation a function of the abundance or scarcity of foreign exchange, sudden changes in the prices of our products in the international markets, the laundering of dollars, and the "swallow capital" attracted by the high levels of interest offered by the government. . . . With the differences that are being registered today between the free-market dollar and the official rate, there is a revaluation, the end of protectionism is accelerated, contraband is dangerously stimulated, and a multiple exchange rate is being established.³⁷

The ANDI leader worried that a new tax law would once again change the rules of the game and affect investment decisions in a way counter to the efforts of the businesses to reduce costs and increase competitiveness. He made a plea for coordination between the government and the private sector in these policies.

The traditional method of harvesting bananas (Photo courtesy of the Colombian Information Service.)

The trade associations had clearly recognized the goals of the government in its neoliberal model; however, the government had to change its policy in relation to coffee when it became apparent that, with the revaluation, coffee exporters were losing money. Since in some cases they had already made the commitment, they had to export.[38] On June 28 the government and the leaders of FEDECAFE agreed on a formula, far from neoliberal, to resolve the problem. The mechanism was simple: For each bag of coffee exported in June, 6,400 pesos were contributed to the Fondo Nacional de Café. Since afterwards the dollars earned would be exchanged at a rate of 3 or 4 percent less, the contribution to this fund was reduced to 4,000 pesos per bag, and thus the exporters would not have to assume any of the loss coming from the revaluation.[39]

Of course, there were also benefits from the new policies. Colombians who made foreign trips were now able to take dollars out of the country without limit and bring back as much foreign exchange as they wished. At the same time, commercial financial companies and banks were allowed to buy and sell foreign currency as they wished.[40] The government even began dollar bond funds in which individual Colombians could invest. The funds were so successful that in 1992, using money deposited in them, the government was able to make an early debt payment to the World Bank. In early July 1991 the government accelerated its sales of banks, industrial and commercial enterprises, and public services and eliminated the bureaucratic red tape required to import capital goods for communications, agricultural production, and chemical and pharmaceuticals production.[41]

Thus Colombia entered the brave new neoliberal world, at least to a point. It was obvious that there would be short-term costs. Industrial production was down 3.6 percent during the first three months of 1991, while the GDP was down 5.7 percent and coffee-bean production 27 percent.[42] The Gaviria government

A coal miner in Andean Colombia (Photo courtesy of the Colombian Information Service.)

had anticipated such difficulties but argued that Colombia would eventually be better off because of the neoliberal changes. In addition to the protection for coffee just mentioned, however, another restraint on a completely open policy was in the exchange rate. Sources suggest that a completely free peso by mid-1992 would have been traded at 450 to the U.S. dollar, but the government kept the "free-trade" peso at about 675 because of what that would have done to exporters.[43] All of this caused uncertainty for the private sector, since it was unclear how far the opening up of the economy will go.

Conclusion

The Colombian economy began the 1980s with a general recession (Table 6.2). Among the reasons for this, in addition to low earnings from coffee and drugs, was a decline in consumption due to the failure of wages for the majority of the people to keep up with inflation. Although the average wage is still much lower in Colombia than in the United States (the minimum wage was about US$100 a month in 1982 and since then in most years has at best kept up with inflation), many prices in Bogotá were as high as or higher than those in southern New England. This was particularly the case for clothing and certain foodstuffs. The devaluation of the 1980s changed the costs for those lucky enough to have foreign currency, as devaluation was much higher than inflation, but it did not help Colombians with pesos only.

Further, in the 1980s the legally imported foreign goods and contraband were often no more expensive than comparable Colombian goods, and many Colombians chose the foreign goods on the assumption that they were better-made. Because of the foreign exchange entering the country, the value of the peso was artificially high, and while this encouraged the imports needed to cool off the inflation it also discouraged exports. Colombian textiles were no longer competitive in the world market.

Investments increasingly were going into areas with good guarantees against inflation—real estate, construction, and financial speculation—rather than productive industry. Capital goods were becoming obsolete and therefore no longer competitive in the world market (although it should be pointed out that modernizing the production of capital goods would have been capital-intensive, increasing unemployment). The opening up of the economy intended by the Barco government was supposed to be gradual so that local industry could prepare. The Gaviria policy, in contrast, did not give industry time to do so. Finally, increasing protectionism in the industrial world in the 1980s made it more difficult to sell goods, especially industrial ones. At the same time, the capital goods needed from the inflation-ridden developed world cost more each year.

At a more basic level, the 1980–1981 recession and the 1988–1992 opening can both be explained as reflections of the dependent position of Colombia in the world economy. In the case of the recession, the industrial world was in recession

TABLE 6.2   The Colombian Economy in the 1980s and 1990s

Year	Unemploy-ment (%)	Growth GDP (%)	Inflation (%)	Devaluation (%)	Coffee Price (US$)	Commercial Balance (US$ Billions)	Foreign Debt (US$ Billions)
1980	9.1	4.1	25.8	15.7	1.56	−.7175	6.457
1981	7.1	2.3	26.4	16.0	1.30	−2.2427	8.518
1982	8.8	0.9	24.0	19.0	1.42	−2.3827	10.269
1983	12.4	1.6	16.6	26.3	1.34	−1.8871	11.458
1984	13.3	3.4	18.3	28.3	1.46	−1.0092	12.350
1985	13.0	3.1	22.4	51.2	1.47	−.5788	14.063
1986	12.5	5.1	21.0	27.2	2.04	+1.2558	14.987
1987	10.1	5.4	24.0	20.4	1.24	+.7964	15.663
1988	10.2	3.7	28.1	27.4	1.67	+.0209	16.434
1989	8.7	3.5	24.3	29.0	0.08	+.4609	17.000
1990	10.6	4.2	32.4	–	–	+1.563	14.498
1991	9.3	2.3	26.8	–	–	±2.959	13.533
1992	9.7	3.3	25.1	–	–	±1.233–	12.926
1993	7.9	5.2	22.6	–	–	±1.298	12.962

SOURCES: *El Espectador* (Bogotá), December 24, 1989; *New York Times*, August 9, 1993; *Colombia Today* 26, 3; 26, 4; 26, 10 (1992); Louis Alberto Moreno, ed., *Síntesis '94 Anuario Social, Politico y Económico de Colombia.*

and therefore Colombia would have to be also. The fragile Colombian economy had historically prospered when there was good, steady, moderate demand for its primary products (whether coffee, marijuana, or cocaine) but not when there was declining demand or even excessive demand. It had never been entirely outwardly oriented (a textile industry, for example, had flourished) but its dependent position meant that short-term considerations such as controlling inflation received priority over long-term development goals (such as protecting national industry). The neoliberal changes also reflect dependency, being instituted as a response to the U.S. government's promise of liberalized trade with countries in the Americas that followed the formula.

Economic conditions were improving by the late 1980s, however, even before the opening began. The causes were primarily exogenous to Colombia: The world recession ended, leading to higher demand for Colombian products; exports of petroleum and coal added to the export base; IMF monitoring led to a lower value for the peso, encouraging exports and discouraging imports. Perhaps most important, the growing demand for Colombian cocaine helped the economy. Colombia had, in effect, found a product with the economic characteristics that all Latin American countries had searched for at least since the Great Depression, one that was price-inelastic and had value added. Coca leaves were for the most part imported from Peru and Bolivia for refinement into cocaine, for which there was a ready market in the United States and Western Europe no matter how high the price. The cocaine industry had a greater "trickle-down" effect than legal industries, and Pablo Escobar and the Ochoa brothers began to do more for the poor people of Medellín than the government had ever been able to do. The question being debated in Colombia today is whether adopting the neoliberal model was a good decision. This question assumes, perhaps incorrectly, given the international forces now at work, that Barco and Gaviria had a choice in the matter. A more appropriate question might be whether, in the medium run, Colombia's economy will be strong enough to offer legitimate employment to all of its workforce.

Notes

1. Carlos F. Diaz-Alejandro, *Foreign Trade Regimes and Economic Development: Colombia* (New York: National Bureau of Economic Research, 1976), 5, 10.

2. Ibid., 5; *Atlas básico de Colombia*, 6; *Colombia Today* 24, no. 5 (1989):1.

3. R. Albert Berry, "Colombia's Economic Situation and Prospects," paper presented at the U.S. State Department Conference on Colombia, Washington, D.C., November 9, 1981, 1.

4. *El Espectador* (Bogotá), January 17, 1988.

5. *Colombia Today* 23, no. 10 (1988/89).

6. Quoted in Miguel Urrutia, *The Development of the Colombian Labor Movement* (New Haven: Yale University Press, 1969), 6–7.

7. Leal, "Social Classes," 196.

8. Confidential interview with an *Estrategia* journalist, April 20, 1981.

9. A. Eugene Havens, William L. Flinn, and Susana Lastarria-Cornhill, "Agrarian Reform and the National Front: A Class Analysis," in Berry, Hellman, and Solaún, eds. *Politics of Compromise: Coalition Government in Colombia* (New Brunswick, N.J.: Transaction Books, 1980), p. 355.

10. Subcommittee on American Republics Affairs, Committee on Foreign Relations, U.S. Senate, *Survey of the Alliance for Progress, Colombia: A Case History of U.S. Aid* (Washington, D.C.: Government Printing Office, 1969), 121.

11. Diaz-Alejandro, *Foreign Trade Regimes*, 29, 61–62.

12. Ibid., 37.

13. François J. Lombard, *The Foreign Investment Screening Process in LDCs: The Case of Colombia, 1967–1975* (Boulder: Westview Press, 1979), 41.

14. Ibid., 28–29.

15. Bagley, "Political Power, Public Policy, and the State," Chapter 3.

16. William Paul McGreevey, "Population Policy Under the National Front," in Berry, Hellman, and Solaún, *Politics of Compromise*, 418.

17. *El Espectador* (Bogotá), July 11, 1991.

18. *El Tiempo* (Bogotá), July 11, 1991.

19. McGreevey, "Population Policy," 418–420. He argues that the National Front, which brought the church behind both parties, made this policy possible.

20. Bagley, "Political Power, Public Policy, and the State," Chapter 5.

21. Ibid.

22. Quoted in John Sheahan, *Aspects of Planning and Development in Colombia*, Technical Papers Series no. 10 (Austin, Tex.: The Institute of Latin American Studies, 1979), 23–24.

23. Malcolm Gillis and Charles E. McLure Jr., "The 1974 Colombian Tax Reform and Income Distribution," in R. Albert Berry and Ronald Soligo (eds.), *Economic Policy and Income Distribution in Colombia* (Boulder: Westview Press, 1980), 47–48.

24. Ministerio de Minas y Energía, *Bases para un plan energético nacional* (Bogotá: n.p., 1977), Table 16.

25. Confidential interview with a former ECOPETROL official, April 24, 1981.

26. Ministerio de Minas y Energía, *Bases para un plan,* Table 16.

27. Jorge Villegas, *Petróleo, oligarquía e imperio* (Bogotá: Ediciones E.S.E., 1969).

28. A more complete account is Harvey F. Kline, "The Coal of 'El Cerrejón': An Historical Analysis of Major Colombian Policy Decisions and MNC Activities," *Inter-American Economic Affairs* 35 (1981):69–90.

29. See Harvey F. Kline, *The Coal of El Cerrejón: Dependent Bargaining and Colombian Policy-Making* (University Park: Pennsylvania State University Press, 1987).

30. Bagley, "Colombia and the War on Drugs," 79–81.

31. Harvey F. Kline, *Energy Policy and the Colombian Elite: A Synthesis and Interpretation,* Center for Hemisphere Studies Occasional Paper no. 4 (Washington, D.C.: American Enterprise Institute, 1982). See also *Exxon and Colombian Coal: An Analysis of the North Cerrejón Debates,* Occasional Papers Series no. 14 (Amherst: Program in Latin American Studies, University of Massachusetts at Amherst, 1982).

32. Confidential interview with a former minister of the treasury, April 20, 1981.

33. Calculated from INTERCOR, "Commercial Declaration" (July 1, 1980), Appendix V, Table 1.

34. *Colombia Today* 24, no. 3 (1989).

35. *El Tiempo* (Bogotá), June 25, 1991.

36. *El Tiempo* (Bogotá), July 9, 1991.

37. *El Espectador* (Bogotá), June 26, 1991.

38. *El Tiempo* (Bogotá), June 29, 1991, my translation.

39. *El Espectador* (Bogotá), June 27, 1991.

40. *El Espectador* (Bogotá), July 3, 1991.

41. *El Tiempo* (Bogotá), July 5, 1991.

42. *El Tiempo* (Bogotá), July 9, 1991; *El Espectador* (Bogotá), July 9, 1991.

43. *El Espectador* (Bogotá), July 9, 1991.

7

THE INTERNATIONAL DIMENSION

RARELY DO INTERNATIONAL ISSUES PLAY an important role in Colombian domestic politics. In part this is because Colombia's economy is not as dominated by
foreign companies as other Latin American economies (Cuba's before the Castro
revolution, for example) and its major export product is not controlled by a few
foreign businesses (as Chilean copper was dominated by Kennecott and An-
aconda before 1970). In part it is because, since the early years of this century, relations between the Colombian government and the U.S. government have been
cordial. There is, however, no reason to deny that Colombia is a relatively small
and poor country in a hemisphere dominated by the United States.

The simplest description of the Colombian foreign-policy establishment is as
weak and diffuse. Up to the present, foreign policy has been made not only in the
Foreign-Affairs Ministry but also in PROEXPO (if the issue was exports),
INCOMEX (imports), or the Treasury (foreign loans and finance). President
Gaviria did add a minister of foreign commerce, and to an extent this position
provides additional coordination. However, the negotiation of foreign treaties
dealing with the most important Colombian export, coffee, has been handled by
the FEDECAFE—a striking indication of the extent of "privatization" of
Colombian policymaking. The Colombian military has a separate network of information and communications. The Colombian embassy in Washington has
only a handful of officials other than clerical and maintenance staff.[1]

In contrast, the United States has a large, centralized foreign-affairs establishment in Colombia. There are approximately two hundred officials in the block-

square embassy in Bogotá (which, Colombian myth has it, was constructed completely with materials imported from the United States and includes secret escape tunnels), including foreign-service officers, Drug Enforcement Agency people, military attachés, and even officials of the Agency for International Development (at least until 1981, although AID programs had been ended, at Colombia's request, in 1975). In addition, there are consulates in Medellín, Cali, and Barranquilla. Despite the size of this staff—and the number of Colombia experts in government agencies in Washington, D.C.—the U.S. government appears to have no clear-cut Colombia policy. Rather its policy seems to be reactive to events within Colombia that affect the United States directly (drugs, for example) and to outside events that impinge on the Andean country. For example, subversion within Colombia (which has been fought, at least since the early 1960s, with U.S. counterinsurgency assistance) has been seen as important as part of a Cuban plan to destabilize the area.

Examination of the history of Colombia's political relations will help explain why foreign affairs have little impact on its domestic politics.

Historical Background

In general the history of Colombian foreign policy is an uneventful one. The only notable occurrence in the nineteenth century was the ill-fated 1826 Congress on Panamá, but it should be remembered that the "Colombia" that called for this congress was Gran Colombia and that the "Colombian" leader involved was the Venezuelan Simón Bolívar. Foreign economic policy was especially designed to exchange Colombian primary products for European (and later U.S.) manufactured goods.

From the Loss of Panamá to the Alliance for Progress

Probably the most important events of Colombian foreign policy came in 1903 when the U.S. government aided and abetted a rebellion in the department of Panamá (which had never been effectively integrated into the economic and political life of the nation). The isthmus had been used for transit for a number of years, and in 1846 the United States and Colombia had signed a treaty for such transit. A railroad had been built. It was only after the Spanish-American War that the U.S. government turned seriously to the question of a canal. For a while there was a debate over whether Mexico, Nicaragua, or Panamá would be the location. When the last of these was chosen, a treaty was negotiated between the United States and Colombia stipulating that Colombia would receive an initial payment of US$10 million and (after ten years) an annual payment of US$250,000 for the right to build the canal. The canal was to be built on a strip of land 10 kilometers

(6.2 miles) in width, and there was a guarantee of Colombian sovereignty over the zone thus created. The treaty was for one hundred years.

The Colombian Senate declined, however, to ratify the treaty. Some senators feared a loss of sovereignty; others argued that the payments were not large enough. The U.S. secretary of state sent a message to the U.S. ambassador, who faithfully passed it on: The Colombians should pass the treaty exactly as negotiated without delay. The attempt to impose this restriction on the Colombian Senate, with its strong tradition of debate, proved the coup de grace for the treaty. Theodore Roosevelt responded with two alternatives: turning to Nicaragua for the canal or intervening in some way "to secure the Panamá route without further dealings with the foolish and homicidal corruptionists in Bogotá."[2] The opportunity for the latter intervention soon came. On November 2, 1903, there was a revolt in Panamá, apparently instigated by the Frenchman Philippe Bunau-Varilla, who had a large investment in the company with the concession to build the canal (although Colombian historian Germán Arciniegas suggests that the U.S. government had prior knowledge).[3] U.S. warships prevented the transit of the Colombian troops sent to put down the revolt. Events then moved with what was for the early twentieth century lightning speed: On November 4 Panamá declared its independence. On November 6 the U.S. government recognized Panamá. On November 13 Bunau-Varilla arrived in Washington to negotiate. On November 15 Secretary of State John Hay gave Bunau-Varilla a draft treaty. On November 17 Bunau-Varilla returned a final draft to Hay, and on November 18 the treaty was signed. Both Bunau-Varilla and Roosevelt later received international awards (TR the Nobel Prize in 1906), and the U.S. president later said, "I took the Canal zone, started the Canal, and then left the U.S. Congress not to debate the Canal, but to debate me."[4] It is little wonder that many Colombians are still sensitive about the incident, as became apparent in 1964 when the U.S. government proposed, among other alternatives, another canal in the Atrato River area of Colombia. An entire generation of Colombians learned their history from a text that concluded its section on the topic with the charge that they, the youth, must rectify their history: "At that time, the cry of Bolívar, inspired by his genius, 'Long Live the God of Colombia!' will be mixed with another, more sonorous and extended, that will make the ashes of Montezuma boil again and give heat and life to the steppes of Patagonia—'Long live the God of Latin America!'"[5] Yet no nationalist movement (such as those later to be very important in Panama itself) was organized in Colombia. One explanation is simply that the opposition party (the Liberals), which might have led such a movement, had been decimated by the War of the Thousand Days.

Although there may have been a chill in Colombian-U.S. relations in the following years, the Conservative presidents of the time faced a clear economic fact: The Colombian economy increasingly depended on export earnings from coffee, and the principal customer for that period was the United States. Conservative

President Marco Fidel Suárez (1918–1921) dignified this relationship when he proclaimed the Doctrine of the Polar Star, by which he meant looking northward, to the powerful United States, both as an example of social and political democracy and as a partner with whom Colombia's destiny was inextricably linked for reasons of geographic proximity and complementary economies.[6] This doctrine has guided Colombian foreign policy ever since.

In 1922 the U.S. Senate ratified the Thompson-Urrutia Treaty, which Colombia had accepted soon after its negotiation in 1914. Under this treaty Colombia was awarded an indemnity of US$25 million for the loss of Panamá. Why the U.S. Senate had waited so long to act seems to be explained by the continuing opposition of Theodore Roosevelt, who had called the treaty a crime against the United States. Roosevelt had died in 1919, and Standard Oil of New Jersey had become interested in acquiring favorable petroleum contracts in Colombia in 1920. In 1924 Colombia won a diplomatic triumph in securing from Peru a boundary settlement that gave it a port on the Amazon River, Leticia, and thereby an outlet to the Atlantic. In 1932 a group of Peruvian irregulars from Iquitos seized the town, thus threatening war between the two countries. Colombia took the matter to the League of Nations, which scolded Peru, and no war eventuated.

During World War II Colombia's policies were unabashedly pro–United States. It was during the immediate prewar and early wartime years that institutionalized military, financial, and technical-cooperation arrangements between the United States and Colombia were first established. Colombia has continued to be a faithful member of inter-American organizations. It is perhaps appropriate that the Organization of American States (OAS) was set up at the 1948 Bogotá Conference and that the first secretary general of the OAS was Alberto Lleras Camargo. In 1994 President César Gaviria was elected secretary general. Further, Colombia was one of the more prominent Latin American participants in the UN's founding San Francisco Conference in 1945. The country's representatives fought against the big-power veto in the Security Council and for a recognized role for regional organizations in the UN Charter.[7]

Colombia was the only Latin American nation to contribute troops to the UN action in Korea. While the Laureano Gómez government may have been motivated by support of the international organization, the sending of troops also reflected the very close relationship that Colombia had developed with the United States. Further, since this action occurred during La Violencia, rumor had it that the first Colombian battalion sent to Korea consisted largely of Liberal troops whom the Conservative administration wanted to keep at a safe distance.[8]

The Alliance for Progress

By the time that John F. Kennedy announced the Alliance for Progress on March 13, 1961, Colombian political leaders had already been calling for a massive assistance program for a decade. Carlos Lleras Restrepo, for example, was one of three experts (along with Eduardo Frei and Raúl Prebisch) charged with the preparation of the 1954 inter-American economic conference, and the proposals of that conference were strikingly similar to those of the Alliance for Progress of seven years later. Further, Colombia had already adopted a land-reform program (at least on paper), one of the explicit goals of the Alliance. Colombia was soon chosen as one of the "showcases" of the Alliance not only for its land reform but also because it had a vigorous private sector, a relatively enlightened political elite, a large industrial base, and many of the typical social and economic problems of Latin America—rapid population growth, a primitive school system, overreliance on one commodity for foreign exchange, and a maldistribution of land and income. The Colombian elite responded, and the country was the first in the Americas to produce a comprehensive plan, a prerequisite for Alliance for Progress assistance.

During the Alliance for Progress years, the U.S. government probably had more influence on Colombian domestic politics than ever before or since. In 1961–1967 U.S. aid was US$732 million (US$491 million of which was Alliance aid administered through AID), and by 1974 the total had reached US$1.4 billion. These monies, closely supervised by AID officials in Bogotá, went into land reform, education, health, housing, transportation, and electricity. There is little doubt that many Colombians benefited from the projects funded by the Alliance for Progress. A report of the Subcommittee on American Republics Affairs of the Committee on Foreign Relations of the U.S. Senate saw the benefits summarized in Table 7.1. But there were "negative externalities" also: Capital-intensive machinery was imported, the tied loans of the Alliance encouraged more trade with the United States, and the country's debt burden increased. Indeed, the same U.S. Senate report concluded that U.S. aid to Colombia made it possible for the Colombian government to postpone making more basic reforms in such fields as public administration, taxation, local government, education, and agriculture. The report concluded that, without Alliance aid, the Colombian government would either have moved more rapidly or faced a revolution (the first of the two alternatives being seen as more likely).[9] Although the short- and medium-term perception might be that the Alliance for Progress was a success, one might ask if the Colombian poor would agree.

In 1975 President Alfonso López Michelsen announced that Colombia would no longer require U.S. economic assistance; he went out of his way to emphasize that although economic relations with the United States existed, "foreign aid breeds an unhealthy economic dependency and delays or undermines measures that should be taken for development."[10] A U.S. diplomat in Colombia complained to me that the embassy had lost all its leverage with the end of AID funding, but certainly that influence did not completely disappear.

The Andean Pact

One of the boldest Colombian initiatives in foreign matters came in the 1960s when the government, along with that of Chile, was instrumental in the instiga-

TABLE 7.1   Quantitative-Indicator Change in Colombia During Alliance for Progress

Indicator	Pre-Alliance[a]	Alliance[b]
Per capita Gross National Product	US$276	US$295
Land reform		
Farms over 100 hectares *(latifundios)*		
% of farms	3.5	2.7
% of total land	66.0	58.9
Farms under 5 hectares *(minifundios)*		
% of farms	62.5	71.4
% of total land	4.5	6.3
Percentage of age-group in school		
Primary	59.9	69.6
Secondary	10.8	16.4
Postsecondary	1.7	2.7
Other indicators (% increase)		
Number of physicians/10,000 people	11.4	10.3
Nurses trained annually	38.6	35.4
Life expectancy at birth	8.5	16.3
Death rate	−11.3	−14.6
Infant mortality	−10.4	−11.8
Number of paved roads	21.2	4.9
Number of gravel roads	28.6	11.0
Number of installed KWH	10.8	32.8

[a]For GNP, 1961; for land reform, 1960; for education, 1961; for other indicators, 1958–1961.
[b]For GNP, 1967; for land reform, 1967; for education, 1966; for other indicators, 1962–1966.
SOURCE: Subcommittee on American Republic Affairs, Committee on Foreign Relations, U.S. Senate, *Survey of the Alliance for Progress: Colombia—A Case History of U.S. Aid* (Washington, D.C.: U.S. Government Printing Office, 1969), passim.

tion of the Andean Common Market (commonly called the Andean Pact). In part the idea resulted from impatience with the slow development of a larger common market through the Latin American Free Trade Association (LAFTA), but rather than replacing LAFTA the Andean Pact was to be a subregional group within it. The concept was first expressed in the Declaration of Bogotá in August 1966 and was formalized in the Agreement of Cartagena in May 1969. The original members of the Andean Pact were Bolivia, Chile, Colombia, Ecuador, and Peru. Venezuela joined in 1973; Chile withdrew in 1975. The pact had seven major goals.

The first of these goals was trade liberalization. All trade barriers between the pact countries were to be eliminated by the end of 1980, with Bolivia and Ecuador having an additional five years to do so. A common external tariff, applicable to imports from outside the subregion, was a second goal, also scheduled to be achieved by 1980. A third was a sectoral program of industrial development. Long lists of which country would produce which goods were drawn up.

A fourth goal was economic policy harmonization—common laws on such things as unfair trade practices, industrial promotion, tourist transit by automobile, and others. A fifth was the creation of a development finance institution (the Andean Development Corporation) with capital from all member countries and from international loans.

No doubt the best-known and most controversial goal of the Andean Pact was a common foreign investment code for investors other than member states or their residents. Decision 24, adopted in 1971, defined as "foreign firms" those in which less than 51 percent of the capital was in the hands of nationals; "mixed companies" were those with 51–80 percent local capital and "national companies" those with 81 percent or more local capital. To take advantage of tariff reductions, foreign companies that existed prior to December 31, 1971, had to declare their intention of becoming mixed enterprises. For new foreign enterprises, gradual conversion to mixed status was mandatory whether they intended to sell in the subregional market or not. Firms intending to export 80 percent or more of their production out of the subregion were exempt from the rule. The reduction of foreign ownership had to be accomplished within twenty-two years in Bolivia and Ecuador. Direct foreign investment would be prohibited in areas already adequately covered by local investors, and so would the purchase of local companies. Foreign investors would remit no more than 14 percent of their investments. Direct foreign investment in insurance companies or banks would be forbidden, and foreign banks would have to offer at least 80 percent of their capital to local investors within a three-year period if they wanted to receive local deposits. Decision 24 did not, however, apply to petroleum or mining. It was suggested that in those areas the form of contract be "joint venture" and that any concessions be short-term ones.

The final goal of the Andean Pact was the creation of Andean multinational enterprises. According to the pact, national investors from the Andean countries would be subject to the provisions of Decision 24 unless they formed such an enterprise, defined as one in which a minimum of 15 percent of the share capital came from at least two member countries.

The results of the Andean Pact were mixed. Trade between the individual nations increased, and there was some specialization of manufacturing industry. Notable successes in Andean multinational enterprises include Monómeros Colombo-Venezolanos, a Colombian and Venezuelan petrochemical joint venture (founded even before Venezuela joined the pact). A reform in Colombia that followed the spirit if not the letter of the pact was the "Colombianization" of the foreign banks. By decree in early 1975 the López government set up a commission to study the question, and the commission met with opposition from the foreign banks but support from Colombian ones. Although according to the Andean Pact foreign banks were required to offer at least 80 percent of their stock to residents of the country, the law approved by the Congress in December 1975 specified that Colombians had to be offered 51 percent of the capital. In effect, the banks were to become mixed enterprises rather than national ones.

During the three years that the law allowed, the foreign banks sold 51 percent of their capital (First National City Bank became the Banco Internacional de Colombia, for example, as all changed their names in so doing). Critics on the left, however, argue that the total capital was also at least doubled in the process: For example, the First National City Bank had paid capital of US$200 million and the Banco Internacional de Colombia had total paid capital of US$448 million. As 49 percent of this latter figure (US$219.5 million) is greater than the "un-Colombianized" bank's paid capital, the critics argue that the López "Colombianization" did not make the country less dependent on foreign banks.[11]

There were always problems with the Andean Pact. For one thing, the laws of several nations (Colombia included) instituting the pact made exceptions to the rules originally agreed upon. For another, transportation difficulties in the Andean region remained an impediment. Perhaps the most notable difficulty, however, came from change of governments. In 1973 the Pinochet military dictatorship replaced the socialist Allende in Chile; in 1980, the democratically elected Belaúnde in Peru called for changes in the pact agreed upon by more progressive military governments in his country.

In Colombia, even in the absence of such dramatic changes of government, there were second thoughts about the stipulations of the Andean Pact. The government of Carlos Lleras Restrepo was the most reformist since the National Front. Although the foreign investment code did not go far beyond Decree-Law 444, it was opposed by interest groups in Colombia, especially ANDI, because it gave "first refusal" to the respective governments in purchasing the stock to be divested by foreign corporations. The opposition surfaced again in November 1981 when an Antioqueño industrialist argued that Decision 24 prevented the entry of additional foreign capital that he thought would help the country.[12]

By the mid-1980s the attitudes of Colombian decisionmakers about the Andean Pact had begun to change. President Betancur argued that it was better to have investment than debt and began to discuss the possibility of withdrawing from the pact along with Ecuador.[13] This trend continued during the Barco years and culminated in the first year of the Gaviria administration. By 1991 foreign investment was again welcomed, including total foreign ownership of banks in Colombia. Decision 24 was simply incompatible with the new neoliberalism. In 1987, through Andean Group Decision 220, member countries were given considerable freedom to choose the rules they wanted to apply to foreign investors. The Barco government, implementing Decree 1265, approved the following framework for foreign companies:

1. The establishment of foreign branches owned completely by the company was again permitted. However, if the branch wished to take advantage of the Andean Pact tariff levels, it had to become a mixed company by transferring at least 15 percent of its equity to Andean investors within three years and 51 percent of its equity in thirty years (up from the fifteen in the original pact).
2. Profits up to 25 percent could be remitted; profits above that level could be reinvested in Colombia as long as a matching amount came from outside the country.
3. Nationals could now sell their participation in companies provided that it was through public offering.
4. Foreign investment was permitted in all sectors of the Colombian economy except public service, communications, television broadcasting, film distribution and exhibition, internal transport of passengers (except for tourism), and the construction of housing.
5. Foreign companies now had access to internal credit lines except long-term development credits. They could also take advantage of export promotion mechanisms and pay royalties to a home company or an overseas affiliate when they pertained to a new technology or one used in the production of export goods.[14]

By 1992 Colombia had established a free-trade zone with Venezuela. The trade between the two countries was expected to reach US$1 billion during the year and, as such, represented 80 percent of the trade between Andean Pact nations. Although transportation difficulties persisted, it seemed likely that such trade would flourish, especially since Venezuelan exports to Colombia might then be reexported to the United States duty-free under the Bush administration's July 1992 Andean Initiative. (Under this initiative, for a ten-year period Colombia, Peru, and Bolivia will be able to export products—except for fabrics, most textile products, sugar, canned tuna, petroleum, and most footwear—to the United States without paying tariffs.) In 1994 a free-trade agreement among Venezuela, Colombia, and Mexico removed all tariff barriers, and high-level officials in both Washington and Bogotá started talking about Colombia's entering the North American Free Trade Agreement.

The Betancur Initiative

In his inaugural address on August 7, 1982, Belisario Betancur announced that his country would follow a nonaligned policy. Colombia became a leading member of the Contadora nations (the others being Venezuela, Mexico, and Panama) seeking negotiated settlements for Central America's civil wars. The basic premise of the Contadora process was that Latin American leaders could understand and help solve the problems of other Latin American countries better than outsiders, including the U.S. government. Betancur reacted to U.S. support of the government of El Salvador and of the contras in Nicaragua as follows: "It is evident that fleets, troops, and foreign advisers in the Central American region, no matter where they come from, contribute nothing to the peace of the region. We have insisted that one of the basic elements for the solution of the Central American crisis is nonintervention in the internal matters of the countries."[15]

In April 1985, for example, Betancur took the Contadora message to Washington, both to the Organization of American States and to President Reagan. After his meeting with the U.S. president, Betancur seemed to endorse "humanitarian" aid to the Nicaraguan contras, and the Reagan administration claimed to have Betancur's support in its effort to get contra aid from Congress. After returning to Bogotá, however, Betancur wrote Reagan arguing for a cease-fire and direct negotiations between the contras and the Sandinista government as soon as posible.[16] Thereafter the Contadora initiative played a less important role in Betancur foreign policy than before. It seems reasonable to conclude that the peace process, and with it Belisario Betancur's desire for a more neutral foreign policy, failed because the superpower of the hemisphere did not want it to succeed.

Colombian Foreign Relations

Intergovernmental Relations

Colombian ties with the U.S. government seem to have become closer in recent years, partly because of the drug trade and partly because of Colombia's problematic relations with Cuba, Nicaragua, and Venezuela, in which it has looked to the United States as a close ally.

Drug Control. During the López Michelsen administration, the U.S. government seemed much more concerned with drug activities than the Colombian government. López saw the problem as a result of the consumption of marijuana and cocaine in the United States rather than of its production in Colombia: "These are North American citizens, with North American capital, with North American registered airplanes, that take off from North American airports to convert us into a drug trafficking platform."[17] The Turbay administration played a more active (and cooperative) role in the control of drug production, perhaps because of the growing realization of the distortions that the illicit trade was bringing into the economy and the increasing drug problems among Colombians. For whatever reason, it entered into a drug-control agreement with the United States involving additional security measures in the Guajira area. For the first time the Colombian military assumed responsibility for drug interdiction (the national police had had this duty) and soon brought the Guajira region under military jurisdiction. The U.S. government provided Colombia with US$3.8 million under the international narcotics program; the police, who had resumed primary responsibility in 1980, were soon seizing three times more marijuana and six times more cocaine than were being confiscated in the United States.[18] In February 1982 U.S. Attorney General

William French claimed that, in fourteen months of a joint Colombian-U.S. operation, 2,594 tonnes (2,860 tons) of marijuana had been seized and more than five hundred people arrested. (Most of the marijuana was seized in Colombia, while most of the arrests were made in the United States.)[19]

Colombian cooperation with the U.S. government in narcotics matters continued during the Betancur and Barco administrations. Despite Betancur's goal of nonalignment in foreign policy, extradition of Colombian drug dealers to the United States continued. After the Galán assassination in 1989, the Barco government received US$65 million in aid from Pentagon stocks for the drug war and, in exchange, continued the extradition. The 1991 Constitution's prohibition of extradition of Colombians clearly did not please the U.S. government. Further, the U.S. ambassador was unhappy with the terms under which Pablo Escobar and other members of the Medellín cartel turned themselves in. At the same time, U.S. representatives seemed to be saying that it might be better for Colombia to punish its own citizens for these crimes; the question was whether it would punish drug dealers as much as the U.S. government thought it should. When Escobar escaped from prison in July 1992, many Colombians feared U.S. intervention to recapture him— a notion that received some support in the U.S. Congress. However, the Bush administration maintained that Colombia should develop its own judicial system.

Disputes with Nicaragua. Colombia and Nicaragua have long contended over the islands of San Andrés and Providencia and the uninhabited keys of Quito Sueño, Roncador, and Serrana. This dispute dates back to 1803, when the reefs and islands were taken away from the captaincy general of Guatemala and placed under the viceroyalty of Nueva Granada. In 1828 Colombia and Nicaragua signed a treaty whereby Colombia recognized Nicaragua's claims to its eastern seaboard (which had also been placed under Nueva Granada's jurisdiction in 1803) in return for Colombian sovereignty over the disputed keys. Colombia's claims to San Andrés and Providencia were based on a treaty between the two nations in 1928 that was not ratified by Nicaragua until 1950. The 1928 treaty did not mention the three keys because they were the subject of litigation between the United States and Colombia. The United States renounced all claims to the reefs in a 1972 treaty, at which point the Somoza government of Nicaragua issued a formal statement reiterating its claims to Quita Sueño, Roncador, and Serrana.[20] Colombia ratified the 1972 treaty in 1973, but it was not until late 1981 that the U.S. Senate followed suit.

In late 1979 the new Sandinista government in Nicaragua reasserted its claim to the keys and the two islands, claiming that Nicaragua's 1928 treaty with Colombia was invalid because it was signed under duress during the U.S. military occupation of Nicaragua. Discussions in March 1982 between the governments of the United States and Colombia of the possibility of a U.S. base on San Andrés,[21] so close to Nicaragua, did nothing to reduce the tension between the two Latin American countries. In late 1983 the issue reemerged when recently published maps of Nicaragua in that country included the disputed islands as part of their territory. But larger issues were to replace this one.

Relations with Cuba. The Colombian government went along with the Rio Treaty nations' vote to end diplomatic relations with Cuba in 1962 and did not reestablish diplomatic ties until 1975. In March 1981, following the M-19 invasion of southern Nariño, the Turbay government broke those ties because some of the guerrillas reported that they had been trained in Cuba. In October 1981 Turbay referred to an "international plot against the democratic regimes of the continent coordinated by Cuba but inspired by other powers."[22] In January 1982 Foreign Minister Carlos Lemos Simmonds added that "Cuba has connections with the drug traffickers and through them sends arms to the armed groups."[23] The U.S. government, likewise, indicated at various times in 1981 and 1982 that Colombia was one of the victims of Cuban aggression.

It was not until July 1991 that consular relations were reestablished between Colombia and Cuba, and the renewal of diplomatic ties took two years more. Given the disintegration of the former Soviet Union and Cuba's serious economic problems, the Communist island was unlikely to support Colombian guerrillas as it had in the past. Indeed, by mid-1994 the Colombian government was talking about petroleum exports to the island nation.

Venezuelan Issues. Bilateral relations with Venezuela differ from those with Nicaragua and Cuba in at least three ways: Both nations are allies of the United States, Colombian-Venezuelan hostilities are deep-seated, and the issues in contention are potentially more important. The first of these issues is illegal immigration. Thousands of Colombians (some estimates are as high as 1 million) are illegally living in Venezuela, where, not unlike illegal Mexican immigrants to the United States, they do menial jobs that others might not; Venezuela is a prosperous "escape valve" for Colombia. Given the long border that the two nations share, it is practically impossible to stop this migration. The second issue is disputed boundaries—the offshore boundary between the two countries in the Gulf of Venezuela, thought to have petroleum, and the boundary between the Colombian department of Guajira and the Venezuelan state of Zulia, which assumed greater importance for Colombians with the exploitation of El Cerrejón coal. During the 1981 Christmas season, a Colombian music group was jailed in Venezuela for playing a "pop" version of the Venezuelan national anthem, and later a group of Venezuelan musicians suffered a kind of revenge in Colombia. More seriously, Colombian leaders worried about the F-16 fighters that the United States had sold to Venezuela, and Venezuelan leaders worried when Colombian guerrilla groups crossed their border. Yet, as we have seen, as the new trade possibilities opened in the 1990s Colombians and Venezuelans put past difficulties aside.

The International Political Economy

Multinational Corporations. According to a study in the mid-1970s, Colombia was seventh in multinational investment in the area (despite being, at the time, fourth in population), behind Brazil, Mexico, Venezuela, Panama, Peru, and Argentina. Only 3.9 percent of such investment in Latin America in 1975 went to Colombia.[24] The investment was US$648 million in 1975, while new investment approved was US$67 million in 1978, US$235 million in 1979, and US$396 million in 1980. Most of the investment in this last year (US$1.249 billion) was Exxon's contribution to the North Cerrejón project. Thus foreign investment was 90 percent in mining, 8.5 percent in manufacturing, and 1.5 percent in financial institutions.[25]

U.S. investment levels were highest in the first half of the 1980s, especially with the Exxon coal investment and the large investment by Occidental Petroleum in the Orinoco Plains. In the first five months of 1991, in contrast, U.S. investment was US$74 million, as compared with US$76 million in 1990. The decline had begun years before, and in 1990 foreign investment declined overall despite the fact that there were fewer controls on foreign investment than before. The head of the DNP, Armando Montenegro, said, "The truth is that although tax and exchange advantages exist, foreign investors are frightened by the terrorism of the first half of the year and by the uncertainty of the constitutional reform." In his opinion, once the new rules were understood there would be an important increase.[26] Under the new exchange rules that began in October 1991, foreign investment funds could enter Colombia through banks or any financial institution, and profits could be remitted through the same organizations. The paperwork of Decree-Law 444 and of Decision 24 of the Andean Pact had been eliminated. Foreign investment was awaited.

Foreign investment tends to be concentrated in certain sectors—according to some Colombian radicals the most profitable ones. Moreover, Colombia firms pay for the use of foreign trademarks and charge more for apparel that bears them.[27] Finally, there is some evidence that several foreign firms, particularly in pharmaceuticals and rubber products, have participated in "transfer pricing." Through the juggling of accounts, which is at least theoretically possible for vertically integrated multinationals, profit-remittance limits have been ignored.

The U.S. embassy plays an active role in promoting the multinationals. One U.S. diplomat said, "What this country needs is more multinational corporations, not fewer. The Colombians are not capable of doing anything by themselves."[28] The embassy serves as host to U.S. businesses that come to Colombia to sell their wares. A representative of the U.S. Department of Energy, speaking in Bogotá, under the embassy's sponsorship, advised Colombians interested in the liquefaction and gasification of coal to "watch what the U.S. companies are doing and choose the technology which suits your needs most."[29] It is only among Colombian radicals that appropriate technology (which for Colombia would be more labor-intensive) is discussed. Among the leaders of the country it is generally assumed that foreign companies are needed because of Colombia's lack of capital, technology, and know-how.

Multilateral Agencies. Although Colombia has not had the debt problem that other Latin American countries have had, as early as 1981 the size of its debt was the subject of debate. One side pointed out that Colombia was the world's fifth-largest debtor, with a total foreign debt that had risen from US$2.350 billion in 1975 to US$3.9 billion in 1980. The government replied that the total foreign debt was less than the country's international reserves (which were about US$5.5 billion) and that the debt service for 1981 would be US$777.1 million, only 13.2 percent of the country's exports. Further, the chief of the DNP reported that debt service for 1986 would be only 19 percent of projected exports, still below the 20–25 percent that international lending agencies considered a maximum.[30]

No single lending agency was dominant as the AID had been during the Alliance for Progress years. Colombia received foreign loans from a multiplicity of sources, including multilateral banks, private banks in the United States and Western Europe, and the export promotion agencies of the governments of the United States, Germany, Canada, and the Soviet Union, among others. These loans were possible simply because Colombia's credit rating was so good. This was dramatically stated by the president of the Inter-American Development Bank in April 1981:

> I always have said in every forum where the general situation in Latin America is analyzed that there is a rare country among us, a country that has in monetary reserves the equivalent of its entire public debt—a country that has completely open credit and has not begun to use it—and that country is Colombia.[31]

In 1966 there was a major confrontation between President Lleras Restrepo and the IMF over the latter's insistence on a major devaluation of the peso. The World Bank, which had major funding programs for Colombia for the past twenty years, particularly in hydroelectricity, has been criticized for its insistence that electricity rates approximate international prices whatever their "real" costs. Even these critics of the World Bank and the IMF (not all of whom are radicals) were forced to reconsider when it became public knowledge that, on the initiative of the World Bank, the Colombian government had asked for a loan from the United Nations to pay for international consultants for CARBOCOL. As it turned out, these consultants (supervised by the World Bank and paid by the United Nations) helped give CARBOCOL officials the technical expertise to deal with Exxon on even terms in the North Cerrejón project.

Colombia was the only Latin American country receiving "new" loans during the 1980s, most commonly from consortia of private banks. Unlike other Latin American countries, it never had to go to the IMF for a standby loan. But, as we have seen, beginning with the Betancur government it was "monitored" by the IMF. By 1991 the total foreign debt had reached US$17 billion still one of the smallest per capita in Latin America. By late in that year international reserves had reached over US$5 billion again.

Colombia in the International Arena

Colombia has never been strongly anti–United States in its international policy. In economic relations Colombian governments have gone along with the conditions imposed by the international lending agencies and have welcomed foreign businesses, although with more strings during the Andean Pact years. Some leaders have even proudly declared that no foreign business interest has been nationalized, unless one counts the "Colombianization" of the banks. The reason for this seems to be that Colombian political leaders are products of a class system. Whereas economic dependency may well have hampered the country's development, these economic elites are doing very well and have never had any reason to use nationalism as a tool for garnering votes. In the 1980s only the Colombian Communist party (which at most gets about 1 percent of the vote), the Rojas ANAPO (for a while), and Galán's New Liberalism raised foreign-policy issues in electoral campaigns. The Liberals and the Conservatives—with their popular bases made secure in other ways—rarely resorted to anti-U.S. populism. In the 1994 presidential campaign, for example, Ernesto Samper and Andrés Pastrana both supported President Gaviria's policy of plea-bargaining with the heads of the drug groups, rejecting U.S. criticism in this regard. Both supported the neoliberal changes in foreign trade, albeit with Samper perhaps favoring subsidies for the poor. Candidates who favored a change in foreign policy simply did not make it to the second round.

Notes

1. Daniel L. Premo, "U.S.-Colombian Relations: A Contemporary Perspective" (Chestertown, Md.: Washington College, 1981, mimeographed), 2.

2. Gil, *Latin American–United States Relations*, 126.

3. Germán Arciniegas, *Biografía del Caribe* (Buenos Aires: Editorial Sudamericana, 1963), 430.

4. Gil, *Latin American–United States Relations*, 128.

5. Henao and Arrubla, *Historia de Colombia*, 818.

6. David Bushnell, "Colombia," in Harold Eugene Davis, Larman C. Wilson, and others, *Latin American Foreign Policies: An Analysis* (Baltimore: Johns Hopkins University Press, 1975), 407.

7. Ibid., 409.

8. Premo, "The Armed Forces and Colombian Politics," 9.

9. Subcommittee on American Republic Affairs, Committee on Foreign Relations, U.S. Senate, *Survey of the Alliance for Progress*, 5.

10. Quoted in Premo, "U.S.-Colombian Relations," 22.

11. Silva Colmenares, *Los verdaderos dueños del país*, 152.

12. *El Espectador* (Bogotá), November 8, 1981.

13. *El Espectador* (Bogotá), February 17, 1985.

14. *Colombia Today* 22, no. 5 (1987).

15. *El Espectador* (Bogotá), August 18, 1983, my translation.

16. *El Espectador* (Bogotá), April 19, 1985.

17. Quoted in Richard B. Craig, "Democratic Implications of Illicit Drug Cultivation," 6.

18. Premo, "U.S.-Colombian Relations," 9.

19. *Latin America Weekly Report,* February 19, 1982.

20. Premo, "U.S.-Colombian Relations," 13–14.

21. Ibid., 16.

22. *El Espectador* (Bogotá), October 11, 1981, my translation.

23. *El Espectador* (Bogotá), January 31, 1982.

24. Lombard, *The Foreign Investment Screening Process,* 124.

25. *El Espectador* (Bogotá), May 27, 1981.

26. *El Espectador* (Bogotá), July 4, 1991, my translation.

27. David Morawetz, *Why the Emperor's New Clothes Are Not Made in Colombia* (New York: Oxford University Press, 1981), 57.

28. Confidential interview with a U.S. diplomat, April 9, 1981.

29. Response to question after lecture at Centro Colombo-Americano, Bogotá, December 1, 1980.

30. *El Espectador* (Bogotá), May 29, 1981.

31. *El Tiempo* (Bogotá), April 9, 1981, my translation.

8

PROGNOSIS

COLOMBIA IS POLITICALLY, ECONOMICALLY, and socially complex, and first impressions are deceiving. Liberal democratic pluralists, marxists, and those looking for a corporate society and/or state will find some things about Colombia that reinforce their ideological biases and many others that do not. The experience of other Latin American countries is not a very good model for Colombia's future. Understanding its prospects calls for a recognition of its differences.

The Colombian Model

The Political Regime
One key characteristic of the Colombian political regime, as we have seen, is the two-party system. Although today it may at long last be on the decline, since 1849 almost all of politics has been affected by the two-party division. Indeed, Ruth Bergins Collier and David Collier argue that the decisions about the entry of organized labor into the political arena (which they consider key in the development of all the Latin American countries they have examined) were greatly affected by the two parties that predated organized labor. In Colombia and in Uruguay, they argue,

> the oligarchy was not united in a single bloc. Rather it was split between the two parties which in many periods confronted each other not only in intense electoral competition but in armed conflict. The dynamic of deeply ingrained two-party competition created a major incentive for the electoral mobilization of workers, thus disposing these countries toward more mobilization incorporation periods. At the

131

same time, a long tradition of interparty alliances created the potential for building a strong, bipartisan antireformist coalition that could reunite elements of the oligarchy and limit the scope of incorporation. . . .

In the heritage period of both countries, the vote of the working class in important measure remained tied to the traditional parties, but labor confederations were much less closely linked to the parties, and both countries experienced a significant increase in labor militancy.[1]

Yet we have also seen that "two-party" does not mean a system like that of the United States. Indeed, in most Colombian presidential elections in this century there have been more than two candidates; politics in the Congress has long been more like a multiparty system; party unity has been lacking, and the new constitution is likely to encourage small parties more than ever.

Before 1991 the Colombian polity had never been a liberal democracy, even though periodic elections had been held and after 1974, with the end of the National Front, there was no electoral restraint. Yet until 1991 Article 120 of the Constitution prevented the president from freely choosing a cabinet and bureaucracy. At the same time, the Colombian polity has not been characterized by interest-group pluralism. Although perhaps, comparatively speaking, the right of the government to withhold legal recognition has not been exercised to the extent that it is in other Latin American countries, the threat of withdrawal of recognition has occasionally been used to control labor and peasant organizations. Colombia is politically not a dictatorship but, although the Colombian president is legally prohibited from taking part in the election of his successor, his influence has traditionally played a role in the choice of the candidate of his party. Indeed, it has been argued that during the sectarian period before 1953 there was party *continuismo*; indeed, one might view the National Front as a constitutional exercise in such *continuismo*. Nor is Colombia's a regime that restricts personal liberties as those of Chile and Argentina have been in the recent past. But the 1978 Security Statute did make the executive branch—and the military—more of a force in day-to-day life than at any time since 1958, and Colombian critics, the Organization of American States, and Amnesty International have complained about the violation of human rights.[2]

Although it has been argued that the tradition of violence in Colombian political life originated with the Amerindians or with their Spanish conquerors, it can also be seen as arising from a number of historical choices: to keep the law-enforcement branch of government weak so that it would not be a threat to civilian government; to allow private groups (from the landowners of the nineteenth century to the paramilitaries of the 1980s) to take the place of official law enforcement; to justify violence in the name of political party and, more recently, guerrilla violence; to make religion part of partisan conflict; to pursue coalitions despite partisan violence; to amnesty participants in partisan and guerrilla violence; and to negotiate (through intermediaries) with the drug lords to end their terrorism. At this writing Colombia is trying to reverse these decisions.

The Gaviria government sought to establish a government of laws in a nation that has long had excellent laws but lacked the means to enforce them. The escape of Pablo Escobar, doubtless made possible by bribes, is only the most dramatic illustration of the problem. Thousands of payoffs are being made every day to poorly paid police and bureaucrats—to avoid traffic tickets, to get paperwork processing done more quickly, to evade paying taxes, and for dozens of other things, and in the countryside the paramilitaries and the guerrillas have their own law-enforcement systems. The government's efforts to improve the law-enforcement system include a major study of the national police resulting in notable reforms in recruitment, training, compensation, and promotion policy. By 1994 every municipality in the country was to have a minimum of sixteen police officers and an adequate level of financial support.[3] Meanwhile, millions of Colombians exist uneasily if not precariously with a government that interferes extensively in their lives, limits their freedom of action, and exacts tribute from them in the form of taxes while being unable to guarantee them security from groups outside the law. Other millions of Colombians live uneasily under a justice system set up by guerrillas, drug dealers, or paramilitary squads.

The Economic System

Economically Colombia has never been a liberal-capitalist state; rather, there have been all kinds of formal and informal connections between economic interest groups and the government. Nor has economic policy been primarily that of any single economic school, although many of the policies of the López Michelsen and Turbay administrations were monetarist in tendency. Rather, economic policy has tended to combine features of a number of schools, with state ownership of some industries, foreign ownership of others, and local private ownership of still others. Although this may sound like the Brazilian *tripé*,[4] it is different in that the Colombian state has been the weakest of these three since even before neoliberalism.

In short, the Colombian model is an eclectic one—neither democratic nor dictatorial, neither capitalist, state capitalist, nor socialist. Some see this as its great strength. As *Estrategia Económica y Financiera* (headed by Rodrigo Botero, first minister of the treasury of the López government) put it at the end of 1980,

> Economic policy, which has been gaining a certain intellectual consensus in the country, is an eclectic mixture of market economics and state interventionism in which elements of import substitution coexist with elements of export promotion, protectionism with international competition, the stimulation of a vigorous private sector with the deliberate action of the state as an industrial mover and promoter in certain fields, relative financial liberty internally with exchange controls, stimuli to foreign private investment with strict limits to its behavior, a prudent monetary and fiscal management with deliberate efforts to modify the productive structure of the country. . . . In its political aspect, the model has produced legitimacy in the exercise of government, the ordered, predictable, and periodic transfer of power, and clear

limitations to authority. This in turn has given sufficient continuity to economic and social policy to gain experience, develop institutions, and initiate long-term programs and projects.[5]

To support these arguments, *Estrategia* presented data showing that during the period 1950 to 1980 GDP per capita was growing, infant mortality was going down, life expectancy and literacy were increasing, and the population growth rate was declining.

Others disagreed, maintaining that the state apparatus was one of the weakest in Latin America, that multinational corporations had been allowed to run many key parts of the economy and amass huge profits, that economic policy had suffered from the lack of continuity, and that democracy was but a facade behind which the military really governed. Some even doubted the reliability of the data on which the *Estrategia* argument was based. They argued that, although there had been economic progress in the past twenty years, there would have been more if (1) the state had played a stronger role, (2) the economy had been socialist, or (3) there had been no protective tariffs and Colombian industry had competed with international business. There may be some merit to one or more of these arguments, but neither *Estrategia* nor its critics could prove that they were right. Further, as one of the writers at *Estrategia* pointed out, the Colombian model just described had no predictive power.[6]

Prospects

Continuation of Electoral Government

The experience of the past ten years suggests that neither a leftist revolution nor a military takeover is likely. Some potential for revolution does exist in the country's maldistribution of wealth. However, regionalism has made it difficult for the lower classes to unite behind one or even a few revolutionary leaders. Throughout Colombian history, the Catholic church and the two traditional political parties have been the only nationwide organizations outside of the government.

The church in Colombia has never supported revolutionary movements, and liberation theology is not dominant there. Furthermore, there has never been an obvious target for a leftist movement in Colombia. There is a strong upper class, and the poor in the cities can see the conspicuous consumption of the rich; in many cases, they work for people who have consumer durables far beyond those of the U.S. middle class. Up to now, however, there has been no single focus for their discontent: no Batista, Somoza, or even a Duarte. In the Colombian electoral system, the theoretical possibility that the poor could get together and win elections has served to defuse revolutionary potential. In July 1991 the former guerrilla leader Antonio Navarro called on the ELN and the FARC to abandon their struggle, arguing that the new constitution had removed all justification for violence because everyone could participate in elections.[7]

By 1991 it appeared that the Colombian masses were weary of violence, having had thirty years of it. In July 1991 there were, for the first time in Colombian history, peaceful demonstrations against the violence, especially after the guerrillas' bombing of electrical distribution systems kept citizens from seeing Colombia's national soccer team defeat Brazil in the South American championships for the first time. Finally, the potential foreign support for leftist groups has disappeared. The Soviet Union no longer exists, and Cuba's economic condition is such that it is unlikely to offer the active support that it has in the past. This does not mean that the ELN and the FARC will necessarily stop fighting immediately, but it does suggest that there is little likelihood of their winning the guerrilla war.

Another possibility that has been discussed is that of military dictatorship along the lines of Chile, Argentina, Uruguay, or Brazil—what recently has been called "bureaucratic authoritarianism."[8] Research on the Southern Cone countries indicates that military (as opposed to personal) dictatorship is associated with either the exhaustion of import substitution or the rise of populist movements. Colombia was late in adopting import-substitution industrialization and, further, turned away from it first through Law 444 of 1967 and later through the opening up of the economy by the Barco and Gaviria governments. Moreover, populist movements have never been important in Colombia simply because the lower classes have always been split between the two traditional parties.[9]

The increase in violence in the 1980s led to predictions of a return of the military to power. But violence reached higher levels in 1990 than during the partisan conflict and the military stayed in its barracks. In August 1991 César Gaviria named a civilian as minister of defense, and again the military stayed in its barracks. In short, there appears no military threat to Colombia elective government.

Perhaps the most likely possibility, simply because of inertia, is continuing civilian government. Elections will continue but not perhaps between the two traditional parties only; interest groups will continue to have their current bias.

In interpreting the 1991 election results, *Semana* asked, "What New Country?"

> The problem before was the lack of ideological boundaries between the two parties. The problem now is that there are no parties. The electoral map of the country seems to be one of a majority party without electoral unity or ideological consistency and a series of multiparty forces that are even less coherent despite electoral unity. The intent of the reformers of ending bipartisanism was achieved, but in a way opposite to that which was proposed. Instead of three or more comparable forces remaining and ending the dominance of Liberalism, what was achieved was to elevate the latter almost to the status of the only party through the breakup of the former minority party.[10]

The 1994 election results underline the uncertainty. As we have seen, the Liberals remained the majority party in both houses of Congress, and the president was still a Liberal, but it was no longer clear that political parties had any meaning.

Another point of uncertainty is the role of the drug dealers. One U.S. expert has estimated that 10 percent of the members of Colombia's Congress are already tainted by drug money.[11] A videocassette delivered to the government in 1991 purported to show a member of the Constituent Assembly taking a bribe to vote for the prohibition of extradition in the new constitution. Given the wealth of the drug traffickers in a poor country, one might speculate that someday they might be able to control the government through the election of a majority of the members of Congress and even of a president. At this point, however, this seems far-fetched.

A final political uncertainty has to do with the future of the AD-M19. While the Constituent Assembly elections of 1990 led some to say that Colombia had for the first time a real leftist party, the 1994 elections made it clear that this was not the case.

The Economic Future

The economic future of Colombia is perhaps even more uncertain than its political one. A revival of the coffee agreement is far from assured. By mid-1992 Colombian coffee was selling for US$0.60 on the international market, and there were plans to destroy 300,000 hectares of coffee in the next year alone. The price had rebounded to about US$1.00 by mid-1994, but no one knew how long it might stay at that level. Petroleum prices went up during the 1991 Gulf War, but it was unclear for how long. It seemed that the Gaviria government was committed to neoliberalism in the belief that in the long run it would lead to a healthier national economy, but the short- and medium-term perspectives were less clear.

If Colombian industry cannot compete internationally it will be allowed to disappear rather than be protected. When jobs are lost, adherents of the Chicago School will argue that "comparative advantage" allows for the greatest benefit for the greatest number of Colombians. Coffee, petroleum, coal, nickel, and a few other products will be exported with little or no value added, while manufactured consumer goods will be imported. Consumer goods will be less expensive, because of economies of scale and other factors, than they are now, but millions may be unemployed or underemployed. The government will not subsidize those millions of unemployed to maintain its own stability, for such subsidies are not part of the neoliberal model. Close monitoring of the activities of the multinational corporations is a thing of the past, and encouragement of additional foreign investment has already begun. In some cases, exorbitant profits will leave the country. The large Colombian financial groups will not be taxed and controlled to make possible some redistribution of wealth.

Manufacturing growth will be a key goal, because that development will employ more people and Colombian products will have more value added. Of course, the hope is that Colombian manufactures will be competitive in the world market as they have been in the past.

The death of Pablo Escobar and the imprisonment of the Ochoa brothers certainly do not mean the end of cocaine exporting. Groups in Medellín, Cali, and elsewhere may move their operations into Venezuela and Brazil, but they are likely to continue to dominate the industry wherever it is domiciled. If the drug of choice were to change from cocaine to heroin, Colombians would surely be involved, as poppy growing was big business in Colombia by 1991.

Final Words

In the final analysis, economic conditions will be paramount in determining the future course of Colombian politics and society. Colombia will remain a minor player in the global economy, but if it does well under the new model there will be little popular pressure for political change. On July 4, 1991, there was a rush of euphoria as the Constituent Assembly presented the new constitution. After the signing, as the national orchestra played Handel's "Hallelujah Chorus," television viewers saw members of the assembly—men and women, former guerrillas and kidnapping victims, indigenes and members of the *oligarquía,* Roman Catholics and representatives of the evangelical movement—embracing each other. Some seventy Colombians of different backgrounds had learned to get along with each other. Yet the euphoria was short-lived; later that month Bogotá newspapers were reporting on the activities of clean-up squads in Pereira, the president's hometown. Colombians are not so naive as to think that writing a new constitution will automatically take care of their problems. It can be hoped, however, that the constitution can help do the hard work that it will take to make Colombia a better place for all of its citizens.

Notes

1. Collier and Collier, *Shaping the Political Arena,* 748, 754.

2. Comité Permanente por la Defensa de los Derechos Humanos, *Represión y Tortura en Colombia* (Bogotá: Fondo Editorial Suramérica, 1980).

3. Confidential interview with an official in the executive branch of government, Bogotá, July 22, 1992; confidential interview with an official in the executive branch of government, Bogotá, May 30, 1994.

4. Peter Evans, *Dependent Development: The Alliance of Multinational, State, and Local Capital in Brazil* (Princeton: Princeton University Press, 1979).

5. "Observaciones acerca del model colombiano de desarrollo 1958–1980," *Estrategia Económica y Financiera* 38 (October 1980):3, 9–10, my translation.

6. Confidential interview with an *Estrategia* journalist, April 20, 1981.

7. Antonio Navarro, quoted in *El Espectador* (Bogotá), July 6, 1991.

8. This topic is addressed in different ways in two excellent pieces. See Ruhl, "An Alternative to the Bureaucratic-Authoritarian Regime," and Jonathan Hartlyn, "The Impact of a Country's Pre-Industrial Structure and the International System on Political

Regime Type: A Case Study of Colombia," paper presented at the 23rd annual International Studies Association Convention, Cincinnati, Ohio, 1982.

9. *El Espectador* (Bogotá), November 3, 1991.

10. *Semana* (Bogotá), October 29–November 5, 1991.

11. David L. Marcus, "It's the Drug Lords Who Are Winning in Colombia," *Birmingham News* (Birmingham, Ala.), August 2, 1992.

Bibliography

Arciniegas, Germán. *Biografía del Caribe.* Buenos Aires: Editorial Sudamericana, 1963.
——. *The State of Latin America.* Translated by Harriet de Onís. New York: Alfred A. Knopf, 1952.
Atlas básico de Colombia. Bogotá: Instituto Geográfico "Agustín Codazzi," 1980.
Bagley, Bruce Michael. "Beyond the National Front: State and Society in Contemporary Colombia." Paper presented at the U.S. State Department." Conference on Colombia, Washington, D.C., November 9, 1981.
——. "Colombia and the War on Drugs." *Foreign Affairs* 67 (1988):70–92.
——. "Political Power, Public Policy, and the State in Colombia: Case Studies of the Urban and Agrarian Reforms during the National Front, 1958–1974." Ph.D. diss., University of California, Los Angeles, 1979.
Berry, R. Albert. "Colombia's Economic Situation and Prospects." Paper presented at the U.S. State Department Conference on Colombia, Washington, D.C., November 9, 1981.
——, and Ronald Soligo. "The Distribution of Income in Colombia: An Overview." In R. Albert Berry and Ronald Soligo (eds.), *Economic Policy and Income Distribution in Colombia.* Boulder: Westview Press, 1980.
Betancur, Belisario. Lecture at the Universidad de los Andes, 1981.
Bushnell, David. "Colombia." In Harold Eugene Davis, Larman C. Wilson, and others, *Latin American Foreign Policies: An Analysis,* 401–418. Baltimore: Johns Hopkins University Press, 1975.
Camacho Guizado, Alvaro. "El ayer y el hoy de la violencia en Colombia: Continuidades y discontinuidades." *Análisis Política,* no. 12 (January–April 1991): 23–34.
——. "Public and Private Dimensions of Urban Violence in Colombia." In Charles Berquist, Ricardo Peñaranda, and Gonzalo Sánchez (eds.), *Violence in Colombia: The Contemporary Crisis in Historical Perspective,* 241–260. Wilmington, Del.: Scholarly Resources, Inc., 1992.
Collier, David, ed. *The New Authoritarianism in Latin America.* Princeton: Princeton University Press, 1979.
Collier, Ruth Bergins, and David Collier. *Shaping the Political Arena: Critical Junctures, the Labor Movement, and Regime Dynamics in Latin America.* Princeton: Princeton University Press, 1991.
Colmenares, Germán. *Partidos políticos y clases sociales.* Bogotá: Ediciones Universidad de los Andes, 1968.
Colombia Today, 1987–1989.
Comisión de Superación de la Violencia. *Pacificar la paz: Lo que no se ha negociado en los acuerdos de paz.* Bogotá: Instituto de Estudios Políticos y Relaciones Internacionales, 1992.
Comité Permanente por la Defensa de los Derechos Humanos. *Represión y tortura en Colombia.* Bogotá: Fondo Editorial Suramérica, 1980.

Commission for the Study of the Violence. "Organized Violence." In Charles Berquist, Ricardo Peñaranda, and Gonzalo Sánchez (eds.), *Violence in Colombia: The Contemporary Crisis in Historical Perspective*, 261–272. Wilmington, Del.: Scholarly Resources, Inc., 1992.

Craig, Richard B. "Domestic Implications of Illicit Drug Cultivation, Processing, and Trafficking in Colombia." Paper presented at the U.S. State Department Conference on Colombia, Washington, D.C., November 9, 1981.

Cromos (Bogotá), July 19, 1985.

Delpar, Helen. "Aspects of Liberal Factionalism in Colombia, 1875–1885," *Hispanic American Historical Review* 51 (May 1971): pp. 250–271.

Diaz-Alejandro, Carlos F. *Foreign Trade Regimes and Economic Development: Colombia*. New York: National Bureau of Economic Research, 1976.

División de Estudios Económicos, Departamento Administrativo Nacional de Estadística. "El comercio exterior Colombiano en 1979." *Revista Mensual de Estadística* 348 (July 1980):31–51.

Dix, Robert H. *Colombia: The Political Dimensions of Change*. New Haven: Yale University Press, 1967.

———. "Consociational Democracy: The Case of Colombia." *Comparative Politics* 12 (1980):303–321.

El Espectador (Bogotá), May 1981–August 1992.

En qué momento se jodió Colombia. Bogotá: Editorial Oveja Negra, 1990.

Evans, Peter. *Dependent Development: The Alliance of Multinational, State, and Local Capital in Brazil*. Princeton: Princeton University Press, 1979.

Fagg, John Edwin. *Latin America: A General History*. New York: Macmillan, 1963.

Fals Borda, Orlando. *Subversión y cambio social*. Bogotá: Ediciones Tercer Mundo, 1968.

Feldman, Robert A., and Michael E. Moseley. "The Northern Andes." In Jesse D. Jennings (ed.), *Ancient South Americans*. San Francisco: W. H. Freeman, 1983.

Fluharty, Vernon Lee. *Dance of the Millions: Military Rule and Social Revolution in Colombia 1930–1956*. 2nd edn. Pittsburgh: University of Pittsburgh Press, 1966.

Forero de Saade, María Teresa, Leonardo Cañón Ortegón, and Javier Armando Pineda Duque (eds.), *Mujer trabajadora: Nuevo compromiso social*. Bogotá: Instituto de Estudios Sociales Juan Pablo II, 1991.

Fuentes Hernández, Alfredo, and Ricardo Villaveces Pardo. "La liberación actual de importaciones y su perspectiva histórica." *Coyuntura Económica* 6 (June 1976):87–98.

Galán, Luis Carlos. "El nuevo liberalismo." *El Tiempo* (Bogotá), June 8, 1981.

García Márquez, Gabriel. *Cien años de soledad*. Buenos Aires: Editorial Sudamericana, 1967. (Published in English as *One Hundred Years of Solitude*, translated by Gregory Rabassa. [New York: Avon, 1970].)

Gil, Federico. *Latin American–United States Relations*. New York: Harcourt Brace Jovanovich, 1971.

Gillis, Malcolm, and Charles E. McLure Jr. "The 1974 Colombian Tax Reform and Income Distribution." In R. Albert Berry and Ronald Soligo (eds.), *Economic Policy and Income Distribution in Colombia*. Boulder: Westview Press, 1980.

Guzmán Campos, Germán, Orlando Fals Borda, and Eduardo Umaña Luna. *La violencia en Colombia*. 2 vols. Bogotá: Ediciones Tercer Mundo, 1962, 1964.

Harkness, Shirley, and Patricia Pinzón de Lewin. "Women, the Vote, and the Party in the Politics of the Colombian National Front." *Journal of Interamerican Studies and World Affairs* 17 (1975):439–463.

Hartlyn, Jonathan. "Consociational Politics in Colombia: Confrontation and Accommodation in Comparative Perspective." Ph.D. diss., Yale University, 1981.

———. "The Impact of a Country's Pre-Industrial Structure and the International System on Political Regime Type: A Case Study of Colombia." Paper presented at the 23rd Annual International Studies Association Convention, Cincinnati, Ohio, 1982.

———. "Interest Groups and Political Conflict in Colombia: A Retrospective and Prospective View." Paper presented at the U.S. State Department Conference on Colombia, Washington, D.C., November 9, 1981.

———. *The Politics of Coalition Rule in Colombia.* Cambridge: Cambridge University Press, 1988.

Havens, A. Eugene, William L. Flinn, and Susana Lastarria-Cornhill. "Agrarian Reform and the National Front: A Class Analysis," in R. Albert Berry, Ronald G. Hellman, and Mauricio Solaún (eds.), *Politics of Compromise: Coalition Government in Colombia.* 341–379. New Brunswick, N.J.: Transaction Books, 1980.

Henao, Jesús María, and Gerardo Arrubla. *Historia de Colombia.* 8th edn. Bogotá: Talleres Editoriales de la Librería Voluntad, 1967.

Hernández Rodríguez, Guillermo. *La alternación ante el pueblo como constituyente primario.* Bogotá: n.p., 1962.

Hoskin, Gary. "The Colombian Party System: Electoral Domination and System Instability." Paper presented at the U.S. State Department Conference on Colombia, Washington, D.C., November 9, 1981.

Hoskin, Gary, Francisco Leal, Harvey Kline, Dora Rothlisberger, and Armando Borrero. *Estudio del comportamiento legislativo en Colombia.* Bogotá: Editorial Universidad de los Andes, 1975.

"Indicadores sociales." *Coyuntura Social* 6 (June 1992).

INTERCOR (International Colombia Resources Corporation). "Commercial Declaration." July 1, 1980.

Jaramillo Uribe, Jaime. "Etapas y sentido de la historia en Colombia," in Mario Arrubla et al., *Colombia hoy,* 15–51. Bogotá: Siglo Veintiuno Editores, 1980.

Kline, Harvey F. "The Coal of 'El Cerrejón': An Historical Analysis of Major Colombian Policy Decisions and MNC Activities." *Inter-American Economic Affairs* 35 (Winter 1981):69–90.

———. *The Coal of El Cerrejón: Dependent Bargaining and Colombian Policy-Making.* University Park: Pennsylvania State University Press, 1987.

———. "The Cohesion of Political Parties in the Colombian Congress: A Case Study of the 1968 Session." Ph.D. diss., University of Texas, 1970.

———. *Energy Policy and the Colombian Elite: A Synthesis and Interpretation.* Center for Hemispheric Studies, Occasional Paper no. 4. Washington, D.C.: American Enterprise Institute, 1982.

———. *Exxon and Colombian Coal: An Analysis of the North Cerrejón Debate.* Program in Latin American Studies, Occasional Papers Series no. 14. Amherst: University of Massachusetts at Amherst, 1982.

——. "From Rural to Urban Society: The Transformation of Colombian Democracy." In Donald L. Herman (ed.), *Democracy in Latin America: Colombia and Venezuela*, 17–45. New York: Praeger, 1988.

——. "The National Front: Historical Perspective and Overview." In R. Albert Berry, Ronald G. Hellman, and Mauricio Solaún (eds.), *Politics of Compromise: Coalition Government in Colombia*, 59–83. New Brunswick, N.J.: Transaction Books, 1980.

——. "Selección de candidatos." In Gary Hoskin et al., *Estudio del comportamiento legislativo en Colombia*, 169–206. Bogotá: Editorial Universidad de los Andes, 1975.

Latin America Weekly Report, November 1981–February 1982.

Leal Buitrago, Francisco. *Estado y política en Colombia*. Bogotá: Siglo Veintiuno, 1984.

——. "Social Classes, International Trade, and Foreign Capital in Colombia: An Attempt at Historical Interpretation of the Formation of the State, 1819–1935." Ph.D. diss., University of Wisconsin, 1974.

Leal Buitrago, Francisco, and Andrés Dávila Ladrón de Guevara. *Clientelismo: El sistema político y su expresión regional*. Bogotá: Tercer Mundo Editores, 1990.

Leal Buitrago, Francisco, and León Zamosc, eds. *Al filo del caos: Crisis política en la Colombia de los años 80*. Bogotá: Tercer Mundo Editores, 1990.

Levine, Daniel H. *Religion and Politics in Latin America: The Catholic Church in Venezuela and Colombia*. Princeton: Princeton University Press, 1981.

Lleras Camargo, Alberto. *Sus mejores páginas*. Bogotá: n.p., n.d.

Lombard, François J. *The Foreign Investment Screening Process in LDCs: The Case of Colombia, 1967–1975*. Boulder: Westview Press, 1979.

Losada, Rodrigo. "Electoral Participation," in R. Albert Berry, Ronald G. Hellman, and Mauricio Solaún (eds.), *Politics of Compromise: Coalition Government in Colombia*, 87–104. New Brunswick, N.J.: Transaction Books, 1980.

McGreevey, William Paul. "Population Policy Under the National Front," in R. Albert Berry, Ronald G. Hellman, and Mauricio Solaún (eds.), *Politics of Compromise: Coalition Government in Colombia*, 413–432. New Brunswick, N.J.: Transaction Books, 1980.

Marcus, David L. "It's the Drug Lords Who Are Winning in Colombia." *Birmingham News* (Birmingham, Ala.), August 2, 1992.

Martz, John D. *Colombia: A Contemporary Political Survey*. Chapel Hill: University of North Carolina Press, 1962.

Medina Gallego, Carlos. *Autodefensas, paramilitares y narcotráfico en Colombia*. Bogotá: Editorial Documentos Periodísticos, 1990.

Melo, Jorge Orlando. "Los paramilitares y su impacto sobre la política." In Francisco Leal Buitrago and León Zamosc (eds.), *Al filo del caos: Crisis política en la Colombia de los años 80*, 475–514. Bogotá: Tercer Mundo Editores, 1990.

Ministerio de Minas y Energía. *Bases para un plan energético nacional*. Bogotá: n.p., 1977.

Morawetz, David. *Why the Emperor's New Clothes Are Not Made in Colombia*. New York: Oxford University Press, 1981.

Morgan, Martha I., "Constitution Making in a Time of Cholera: Women and the 1991 Colombian Constitution." *Yale Journal of Law and Feminism* 4 (1992):359–361.

"Observaciones acerca del modelo colombiano de desarrollo 1958–1980." *Estrategia Económica y Financiera* 38 (October 1980):5–11.

Oppenheimer, Andres. "Rising Violence Rips Colombia." *Miami Herald*, June 12, 1988.

Oquist, Paul. *Violence, Conflict, and Politics in Colombia*. New York: Academic Press, 1980.

Payne, James L. "The Oligarchy Muddle." *World Politics* 20 (1968):439–453.

———. *Patterns of Conflict in Colombia.* New Haven: Yale University Press, 1968.

Pecaut, Daniel. "Guerrillas and Violence." In Charles Berquist, Ricardo Peñaranda, and Gonzalo Sánchez (eds.), *Violence in Colombia: The Contemporary Crisis in Historical Perspective,* 217–240. Wilmington, Del.: Scholarly Resources, Inc., 1992.

Pizarro, Eduardo. "Revolutionary Guerrilla Groups in Colombia." In Charles Berquist, Ricardo Peñaranda, and Gonzalo Sánchez (eds.), *Violence in Colombia: The Contemporary Crisis in Historical Perspective,* 169–194. Wilmington, Del.: Scholarly Resources, Inc., 1992.

Premo, Daniel L. "The Armed Forces and Colombian Politics: In Search of a Mission." Chestertown, Md.: Washington College, 1981. Mimeographed.

"Profile: Prostitutes in Bogotá." *Hemisphere* 5 (Fall 1992):31.

Ramírez Moreno, Augusto. *La crisis del Partido Conservador.* Bogota: n.p., 1937.

Ramón, Justo, S. C. *Historia de Colombia: Significado de su obra colonial, independencia y república.* Bogotá: n.p., 1962.

———. "U.S.-Colombian Relations: A Contemporary Perspective." Chestertown, Md.: Washington College, 1981. Mimeographed.

Reichel-Dolmatoff, Gerardo. *Ancient People and Places: Colombia.* New York: Praeger, 1965.

Restrepo, Luís Alberto. "The Crisis of the Current Political Regime and Its Possible Outcomes." In Charles Berquist, Ricardo Peñaranda, and Gonzalo Sánchez (eds.), *Violence in Colombia: The Contemporary Crisis in Historical Perspective,* 273–292. Wilmington, Del.: Scholarly Resources, Inc., 1992.

Rippy, J. Fred. *The Capitalists and Colombia.* New York: Vanguard Press, 1931.

Rivera Ortiz, Angel Israel. "The Politics of Development Planning in Colombia." Ph.D. diss., State University of New York at Buffalo, 1976.

Ruhl, J. Mark. "An Alternative to the Bureaucratic-Authoritarian Regime: The Case of Colombian Modernization." *Inter-American Economic Affairs* 35 (1981):43–69.

———. "Civil-Military Relations in Colombia: A Societal Explanation." *Journal of Interamerican Studies and World Affairs* 23 (1981):123–146.

———. *Colombia: Armed Forces and Society.* Syracuse University Foreign and Comparative Studies Program, Latin American Series, no. 1. Syracuse: Syracuse University, 1980.

Sánchez, Gonzalo. "The Violence: An Interpretative Synthesis." In Charles Berquist, Ricardo Peñaranda, and Gonzalo Sánchez (eds.), *Violence in Colombia: The Contemporary Crisis in Historical Perspective,* 75–124. Wilmington, Del.: Scholarly Resources, Inc., 1992.

Santa, Eduardo. *Sociología política de Colombia.* Bogotá: Ediciones Tercer Mundo, 1964.

Semana (Bogotá), July 1990–May 1992.

Sharpless, Richard E. *Gaitán of Colombia: A Political Biography.* Pittsburgh: University of Pittsburgh Press, 1978.

Sheahan, John. *Aspects of Planning and Development in Colombia.* Technical Paper Series no. 10. Austin, Tex.: Institute of Latin American Studies, 1977.

Silva Colmenares, Julio. *Los verdaderos dueños del país.* Bogotá: Fondo Editorial Suramérica, 1977.

Subcommittee on American Republics Affairs, Committee on Foreign Relations, U.S. Senate. *Survey of the Alliance for Progress, Colombia: A Case History of U.S. Aid.* Washington, D.C.: Government Printing Office, 1969.

El Tiempo (Bogotá), March 1981–July 1991.

Urrutia, Miguel. *The Development of the Colombian Labor Movement.* New Haven: Yale University Press, 1969.

——. "Diversidad ideológica e integración Andina." *Coyuntura Económica* 100 (1980): 187–203.

Villegas, Jorge. *Petróleo, oligarquía e imperio.* Bogotá: Ediciones E.S.E., 1969.

Wade, Peter. *Blackness and Race Mixture: The Dynamics of Racial Identity in Colombia.* Baltimore: Johns Hopkins University Press, 1993.

Wilde, Alexander W. "Conversations Among Gentlemen: Oligarchical Democracy in Colombia." In Juan J. Linz and Alfred Stepan (eds.), *The Breakdown of Democratic Regimes: Latin America,* 28–81. Baltimore: Johns Hopkins University Press, 1978.

Williams, Miles Wendell. "El Frente Nacional: Colombia's Experiment in Controlled Democracy." Ph.D. diss., Vanderbilt University, 1972.

About the Book and Author

Although Colombia is the third-largest country in Latin America, it has been little known until recent years and does not fit many of the patterns common to other countries in the region. Competition between political parties, for example, has always been more important than class conflict; there is no tradition of military dictatorship; and corporatist structures are weak. Over the past decade, however, Colombia has gained notoriety, principally as the supplier of 80 percent of the cocaine consumed in the United States.

The second edition of this comprehensive country profile begins with a discussion of the blend of Andean and Caribbean characteristics that define Colombia, particularly in its geography, demography, and social structure. The author then presents a detailed political history that extends from before the arrival of the Spanish, including a portrait of early Amerindian populations, and continues through the turbulence of guerrilla, drug, and paramilitary violence in the 1980s and constitutional reforms of the 1990s. Harvey Kline argues that Colombia is now conscientiously attempting to alter historical patterns that have led it to play a key role in the international drug trade and to lead the world in the rate of homicides. A chapter on the economy offers a historical analysis of its evolution and examines economic and trade policies of recent presidents. Finally, the author looks at the international dimension of Colombian politics, especially its long-standing relationship with the United States and its increasingly important regional ties.

Harvey F. Kline is professor of political science and director of the Latin American Studies Program at the University of Alabama–Tuscaloosa.

Index